English is very widely spok

Mountainous.

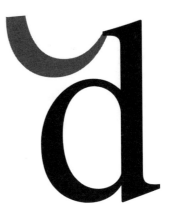

AVALON
Direct English

SECOND EDITION

Book 1
Student's Book

에듀록

| General Editor | Tor Nicol |
| Co-editor | Andrew Leishman |

Andrew Day
Mark El Kadhi
Jeff Goldenberg
Natasha Bolonkin
Laura Markovitz

| Cover design | Stephen Portman |
| | Andrew Leishman |

Published by

AVALON
Book Company

Thanks

We would like to thank all the teachers at Avalon School of English, London, whose comments on the first edition were invaluable.

Many thanks to the teachers who taught the second edition, in particular, Micheline Tzwern and Emma Barrett, whose comments and criticisms were appreciated.

Special thanks to Natasha Bolonkin who corrected the proofs.

Published by **The Avalon Book Company Limited**.
8 Denmark Street, London WC2H 8LS

© Avalon Book Company, Limited, 1999

Printed in the UK by Biddles Ltd, Guildford.

General Contents

Grammar Contents

Unit 1

Hello   **My name is ...**

What is ...?   **Your name is ...**

Q. Hello, my name is ... What is your name ?
A. My name is ...

Q. What is my name ?
A. Your name is ...

Q. What is your name ?*
A. My name is ...

What is it ?   *n.* **a pencil**   *n.* **a pen**   *n.* **a book**

It is a pencil.   It is a pen.   It is a book.

Q. What is it ?
A. It is a pencil.

Q. What is it ?
A. It is a pen.

Q. What is it ?
A. It is a book.

n. **a table**   *n.* **a chair**   *n.* **a picture**

Q. What is it ?
A. It is a table.

Q. What is it ?
A. It is a ...

n. **a door**   *n.* **a light**   *n.* **a window**

Q. What is it ?
A. It is a ...

n. **a floor**   *n.* **a wall**   *n.* **a ceiling**

Q. What is it ?
A. It is a ...

Is it a ...?   **Yes it is a ...**

Q. Is it a book ?
A. Yes, it is a book.

Q. Is it a pen ?
A. Yes, it is a pen.

Q. Is it a ... ?
A. Yes, it is a ...

my   your   his   her

Q. What is your name ?

Q. What is my name ?

Q. What is his name ?

Q. What is her name ?

Q. Is my name ... ?
A. Yes, your name is ...

Q. Is your name ... ?
A. Yes, my name is ...

Q. Is his / her name ... ?
A. Yes, his / her name is ...

v. **to be**   *n.* **a student**   *n.* **a teacher**
                        n. **a man**   *n.* **a woman**

I am   I am a **teacher**.
you are   You are a **student**.
he is   He is a **man**.
she is   She is a **woman**.
it is   It is a **pen**.

Q. Are you a student ?
A. Yes, I am a student.

Q. Am I a teacher ?
A. Yes, you are a teacher.

Q. Is he/she a student ?
A. Yes, he/she is a student.

Q. Is he a man ?
A. Yes, he is a man.

Q. Is she a woman ?
A. Yes, she is a woman.

numbers

n. **number**

1	one	6	six
2	two	7	seven
3	three	8	eight
4	four	9	nine
5	five	10	ten

v. **to count**   **from**...   **to**...   **please**

Q. Count to ten, please.

Q. Count from one to ten, please.

in   **on**
the   *n.* **classroom**

Q. Is the book on the table ?
A. Yes, the book is on the table.

Q. Is the picture on the wall ?

Q. Is the table in the classroom ?

plurals
Book = singular. (1 book)
Books = plural. (2,3,4 ... books)

Q. Is it singular ?

Q. Is it plural ?

singular *to be*	plural *to be*	
I am	**we are**	**We are** in the classroom.
you are	**you are**	**You are** students.
he/she/it is	**they are**	**They are** chairs.

Q. Are we in the classroom ?

Q. Are you students ?

Q. Are they chairs ?

Q. Are they students ?

11	eleven	16	sixteen
12	twelve	17	seventeen
13	thirteen	18	eighteen
14	fourteen	19	nineteen
15	fifteen	20	twenty

Q. Count from eleven to twenty, please.

Q. Count from one to twenty, please.

n. **arm** *n.* **leg** *n.* **hand** *n.* **head***

Q. What is it ?
A. It is your ... (x 4)

Q. What is it ?
A. It is my ...

Q. Is it my/your ... ?

Q. What are they ?

n. **face** *n.* **ears** *n.* **eyes**
n. **nose** *n.* **mouth** *n.* **hair**

Q. What is it ?
A. It is your ... (x 6)

Q. Is it my/your ... ?

question (?)	positive (+)	negative (-)
Am I ...?	I am ...	I am **not** ...
Are you ... ?	You are ...	You are **not** ...
Is he/she ...?	He/She is ...	He/She is **not** ...
Is it ...?	It is ...	It is **not** ...
Are we ... ?	We are ...	We are **not** ...
Are you ... ?	You are...	You are **not** ...
Are they ... ?	They are ...	They are **not** ...

eg. Q. **Is he** a student ?
+A. Yes, **he is** a student.
-A. No, **he is not** a student.

eg. Q. **Are they** books ?
+A. Yes, **they are** books.
-A. No, **they are not** books.

Q. Am I a student ?
A. No, you are not a student.

Q. Are you a teacher ?
A. No, I am not a teacher.

Q. Is it a book ?
A. No, it is not a book.

but

eg.   I am not a student, **but** I am a teacher.
You are not a teacher, **but** you are a student.
It is not a chair, **but** it is a table.

Q. Is it a table ?
A. No, it isn't a table, but it is a chair.

Q. Is it a wall?
A. No, it is not a wall, but it is a table.

Q. Am I a student ?

Q. Are you a teacher ?

Q. Is he a woman ?

Q. Is she a man ?

Q. Are they teachers ?

Where ... ?   **I am from ...**
Where is he from ?   **He is from Japan.**

Q. Where am I from ?
A. You are from

Q. Where are you from ?
A. I am from ...

Q. Where is he from ?
A. He is from ...

Q. Where is she from ?
A. She is from ...

Q. Where is the light ?
A. The light is on the ceiling.

Q. Where is the pen ?
A. The pen is on the table.

Q. Where is the picture ?
A. The picture is on the wall.

prep. **under**   *prep.* **behind**   *prep.* **in front of**   *n.* **bag**

Q. Is the book under the chair ?

Q. Is the bag on the chair ?

Q. Is the table in front of the chair?*
A. Yes ...

Q. Am I behind the table ?
A. Yes ...

Q. Where is your bag ?

Q. Where is your book ?

Q. Where am I ?

or

Q. Is it a pen or a pencil ?
A. It is a ...

Q. Are you are man or a woman ?

Q. Am I a teacher or a student ?

Q. Are you from England or ... ?

Q. Is the pen on the table or under the table ?

n. **city**   *n.* **country**
n. **London**   *n.* **England**
eg.   **London** is a **city.**
       England is a **country.**
       London is in **England.**

Q. Is London a city or a country ?
A. London is a city.

Q. Where is London ?
A. London is in England.

Q. What city are you from ?
Q. Where is ... (name of city)
A. (Name of city) ... is in ...

n. **elephant**   *n.* **mouse**
adj. **big**   *adj.* **small**
An **elephant** is **big** but a **mouse** is **small.**
England is a **small** country but London is a **big** city.

Q. Is an elephant big ?

Q. Is a mouse small ?

Q. Is England a big country or a small country ?

Q. Is London a small city ?

n. **Brazil**   *n.* **Scotland**
adj. **hot**   *adj.* **cold**
Brazil is a big, **hot** country.
Scotland is a small, **cold** country.

Q. Is Brazil a hot country ?

Q. Is Scotland a cold country ?

Q. Is your country hot or cold ?

adj. **black**   *adj.* **white**   *n.* **board**

Q. What is it ?*

Q. Is the board black or white ?

Q. Is it black or white?*

Q. Where is the board ?

adj. **clean**   *adj.* **dirty**

Q. Is the floor clean ?

Q. Is London a dirty city ?

Q. Is your city clean or dirty ?

adj. **left**   *adj.* **right**

Q. Is it my left hand or my right hand ?

Q. Is it my left eye or my right eye ?

Q. Is it his/her left arm ?

the opposite of
The opposite of yes is no.
The opposite of big is small.
The opposite of black is white.
The opposite of clean is dirty.

Q. What is the opposite of big ?
A. The opposite of big is small.

Q. What is the opposite of black ?
A. The opposite of black is white.

Q. What is the opposite of left ?

Q. What is the opposite of hot ?

Q. What is the opposite of clean ?

	there is ...	there are ...	
	question (?)	**positive (+)**	**negative (-)**
singular	Is there a ... ?	Yes, there is a ...	No, there is **not** a ...
plural	Are there ... ?	Yes, there are ...	No there are **not** ...

eg. Q.   Is there a book on the table ?
+A.   Yes, there is a book on the table.
-A.   No, there is **not** a book on the table.

Q.   Are there chairs in the classroom ?
+A.   Yes, there are chairs in the classroom.
-A.   No, there are **not** chairs in the classroom.

Q.   Is there a book on the table ?

Q.   Is there a teacher in the classroom ?

Q.   Are there students in the classroom ?

Q.   Is there a book in my hand ?
A.   No, there is not ...

Q.   Are there books in your bag ?

how many ... ?

Q.	**How many**	books pens windows	**are there ?**

A.   (singular)   **There is** one book/window/pen.
A.   (plural)   **There are** 2,3,4 books / pens / windows.

Q.   How many students are there in the classroom ?
A.   There are ..... students in the classroom.

Q.   How many pictures are there on the wall ?

Q.   How many teachers are there in the classroom ?

Q.   How many chairs are there in the classroom ?

Q.   How many doors are there in the classroom ?

The Alphabet

A B C D **E** F G H **I** J K L M N **O** P Q R S T **U** V W X Y Z

a b c d **e** f g h **i** j k l m n **o** p q r s t **u** v w x y z

n. **alphabet**   *n.* **letter**
There are 26 **letters** in the English **alphabet**

Q. How many letters are there in the English alphabet ?

Q. What are they ?
A. They are a, b, c, ...

n. **word**
"Book" is a **word**
"Dirty" is a **word**.
"Where" is a **word**.
There are four **letters** in the **word** "book".
There are five **letters** in the **word** "dirty."

Q. How many letters are there in the word "BOOK" ?

Q. How many letters are there in the word "WINDOW" ?

Q. How many letters are there in the word "ELEPHANT"?

n. **sentence**
The book is on the table. = **sentence**
There are six **words** in the **sentence** "The book is on the table."

Q. How many words are there in the sentence : "The book is on the table"?

Q. How many words are there in the sentence : "London is a big city"?

Q. How many words are there in the sentence : "The students are in the classroom." ?

n. **vowel**   *n.* **consonant**
There are 5 **vowels** in the English alphabet.
The English **vowels** are : **A,E,I,O,U.**

Q. How many vowels are there in the alphabet ?
A. There are five vowels in the alphabet.

Q. What are the English vowels ?
A. The English vowels are A,E,I,O,U.

Q. Is the letter **a** a vowel ?
A. Yes, the letter **a** is a vowel.

Q. Is the letter **b** a consonant ?
A. Yes, the letter **b** is a consonant.

Q. Is the letter **e** a consonant ?
A. No, the letter **e** is not a consonant, but it is a vowel.

v. **to say**

Q. Say your name.

Q. Say my name.

Q. Say the letters ...
B/V   E/I   P/F   L/R   S/Z   K/Q   G/J   V/W   O/U

v. **to spell**
We **spell** the word "pen", P-E-N.

Q. Say the word window.
Q. Spell the word window.

Q. Say the word country.
Q. Spell the word country.

Q. Say the word ceiling.
Q. Spell the word ceiling.

Q. Say your name.
Q. Spell your name.

n. **day**   *n.* **week**
There are seven **days** in a **week**.
The days of the **week** are :

Monday   **Tuesday**   **Wednesday**   **Thursday**
Friday   **Saturday**   **Sunday**

Q. How many days are there in a week ?

Q. What are the days of the week ?
A. The days of the week are ...

n. **today**

Q. What day is it today ?

Q. Is today Saturday ?

Q. Is it hot or cold today ?

and
Brazil **and** England are countries.
London **and** Paris are cities.

Q. Are London and Paris cities ?

Q. Are 6 and 7 numbers ?

Q. Are A and E vowels ?

Q. Are Monday and Tuesday days of the week ?

between
Tuesday is **between** Monday and Wednesday.
5 is **between** 4 and 6.

Q. Is Tuesday between Monday and Wednesday ?
A. Yes, Tuesday is between Monday and Wednesday.

Q. Is 5 between 4 and 6 ?

Q. Is Y between X and Z ?

before   **after**
Monday is **before** Tuesday.   Wednesday is **after** Tuesday.
A is **before** B.   C is **after** B.

Q. Is Friday before Saturday ?
A. Yes, Friday is before Saturday.

Q. Is Wednesday after Tuesday ?
A. Yes, Wednesday is after Tuesday.

Q. Is A before B ?

Q. Is C after B ?

Q. Is 12 before 13 ?

Q. Is 14 after 13 ?

which ?

Q. Which letter is between A and C ?
A. B is between A and C.

Q. Which day is between Friday and Sunday ?

Q. Which day is before Wednesday ?
A. Tuesday is before Wednesday.

Q. Which day is after Wednesday ?
A. Thursday ...

Q. Which letter is after B ?

Q. Which letter is before B ?

Q. Which number is after 13 ?

Q. Which number is before 13 ?

Who ?

Q. Who are you ?

Q. Who am I ?

Q. Who is he/she ?

Q. Who is in the classroom today ?

Q. Who are your teachers ?

exercise

Yes or no ?

1. Are you a student ? ....
2. Is your teacher a woman ? ....
3. Are you from England ? ....
4. Is there a bag under your chair ? ....
5. Is the word 'book' singular ? ....
6. Is the word 'chairs' singular ? ....
7. Is it Saturday today ? ....
8. Is a mouse a big animal ? ....
9. Is Brazil a hot country ? ....
10. Is yes the opposite of no ? ....

Unit 2

the months of the year

January	**February**	**March**	**April**
May	**June**	**July**	**August**
September	**October**	**November**	**December**

There are 12 **months** in a **year**.

Q. How many months are there in a year ?

Q. What are the months of the year ?
A. The months of the year are ...

Q. Which month is between September and November ? october.

Q. Which month is after April ?

now

Q. Which country are you from ?
Q. Which country are you in now ?

Q. Where is the pen ?
Q. Where is the pen now ?

Q. Is it June now ?

Q. Is it hot or cold in your country now ?

the four seasons

Spring　　　**Summer**　　　**Autumn**　　　**Winter**

Q. What are the four seasons ?

Q. Which season is it now ?

Q. Is it cold in summer ?

Q. Is January in winter ?

Q. Are July and August in winter ?

adj. **first** adj. **last**

eg. A is the **first** letter of the alphabet.
Z is the **last** letter of the alphabet.

Q. What is the first letter of the alphabet ?

Q. What is the last letter of the alphabet ?

Q. What is the last month of the year ?

Q. What is the first day of the week ?

Q. What is the last day of the week ?

Q. What is the first letter of your name ?

a / an n. **umbrella**

We say **a** mouse but we say **an** elephant.
We say **a** book but we say **an** umbrella.
We say '**a**' before a **consonant** but we say '**an**' before a **vowel**

Q. Is a mouse small ?

Q. Is an elephant big ?

Q. Is there an umbrella in the classroom ?

n. **animal** n. **dog** n. **cat**

A cat is **an** animal.
A dog is **an** animal
We say **an** before the word animal - **an** animal

Q. Is a mouse an animal ?

Q. Is a mouse a small animal ?

Q. Is an elephant an animal ?

Q. Is an elephant a small animal ?

Q. Is a dog an animal ?

Q. Is a cat an animal ?

Numbers from 20 to 100

20 = twenty	**30 = thirty**	**40 = forty**
50 = fifty	**60 = sixty**	**70 = seventy**
80 = eighty	**90 = ninety**	**100 = one hundred**

Q. Say the number: 40 82 33 55 71 22

26

n. address
house/ flat number + street / road + city + post code + country

exercise

My address is:

.... (number and street/road)

.... (city)

.... (post code)

.... (country)

Q. What is your address ?

Q. What is the address of this school ?

Q. What is his/her address ?*

n. second   **n. minute**   **n. hour**
eg.   60 seconds = 1 minute
      60 minutes = 1 hour
      24 hours = 1 day *

Q. How many seconds are there in one minute ? There are . 60 Seoondin 1miumte.

Q. How many minutes are there in one hour ?

Q. Are there 24 hours in a day ?

the time

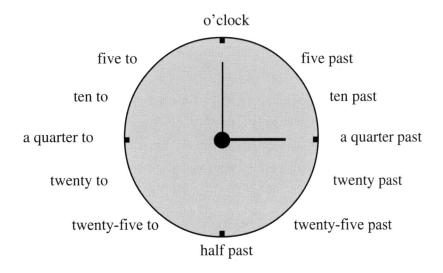

o'clock

five to   five past

ten to   ten past

a quarter to   a quarter past

twenty to   twenty past

twenty-five to   twenty-five past

half past

n. clock   **n. watch**

Q. Is there a clock in the classroom ?

Q. Is a watch big or small ?

Q. Is a clock big or small ?

3.00 = three **o'clock**

Q. What **time** is it ?
A. It is three **o'clock**.

Q. What time is it ?*

3.10 = ten **past** three

It is ten **past** three.

Q. What time is it ?*

3.50 = ten **to** four

It is ten **to** four.

Q. What time is it ?*

1/4 = a quarter   **1/2 = a half**
4.15 = **quarter** past four   4.30 = **half** past four   4.45 = **quarter** to five

Q. What time is it ?*

Q. What time is it now ?*

n. **colour**   **What colour ... ?**

>   **blue   yellow   orange   grey**
>   **red   green   brown   pink**

NB. My chair is blue.
     NOT
     ~~My chair is blue colour.~~

Q. What colour is your chair ?
A. My chair is blue.

Q. What colour is the floor ?

Q. What colour are the chairs ?

Q. What colour is his/her pen ?

Q. Is my book blue ?

Q. Are the walls blue ?

Q. What colour is your hair ?

Q. What colour are your eyes ?

gred   *Porpcle.*

> n. **shoes** *(plural)*   n. **socks** *(plural)*   n. **shirt**
> n. **jumper**   n. **jacket**
> n. **trousers** *(plural)* n. **jeans** *(plural)*
>
> The words trousers and jeans are plural.
> We say his trousers **are** blue, NOT ~~his trousers is blue~~.

Q. What colour are his/her shoes ?
A. His/her shoes are ...

Q. What colour is his/her shirt ?

Q. What colour are his/her trousers ?

Q. What colour are his/her socks ?

Q. What colour is his/her jumper ?

Q. What colour is his/her jacket ?   *is t.*

Q. Is his jacket yellow ?

Q. Are his trousers orange ?

Q. Are they trousers or jeans ?

this   **that**

Q. What colour is this pen ? (teacher's pen)
A. That pen is ...

Q. What colour is that pen ? (student's pen)
A. This pen is ...

Q. Is the board on this wall ? (teacher stands by board)
A. Yes, the board is on that wall.

here   **there**
My book is **here** on the table.
The light is **there** on the ceiling.
We are **here** in this classroom.

Q. My book is here. Where is your book ?
A. My book is here.

Q. Your chair is there. Where is my chair ?
A. Your chair is there.

Q. Where is your pen ?

Q. Where is the door ?

Q. Where is the window ?

Q. Is (student's name) here today ?

Q. Where are you from ?
Q. Is it hot there ?

these
The plural of this is **these**.
eg.   **These** books are blue.

those
The plural of that is **those**.
eg.   **Those** students are from Japan.

Q.   What is the plural of 'this' ?

Q.   What is the plural of 'that' ?

Q.   What colour are these shoes ?

Q.   What colour are those shoes ?

Q.   Are these chairs yellow ?

Whose ?

Q.   Whose pen is this ?
A.   It is your pen.

Q.   Whose book is that ?

Q.   Whose bag is that ?

Q.   Whose shoes are those ?
A.   They are ...

's

Whose book is that ? It is John**'s** book. = It is his book.
Whose pens are those ? They are Anna**'s** pens. = They are her pens.

Q.   Is that ... 's book ?*

Q.   What colour are ... 's shoes ?

Q.   Is this the teacher's chair ?

Q.   What colour are ...'s eyes ?

Q.   What colour is ...'s hair ?

n. **thing**

eg.   This **thing** is a table.*
That **thing** is a light.*

Q.   What is this thing ?*

Q.   What is that thing ?*

Q.   What colour is this thing ?

Q.   What colour is that thing ?

n. **person**

Q. Are you a person or a thing ?

Q. Is it person or a thing ?

Q. Who is that person ?
A. He/She is ...

regular plurals

1 book   3 books
1 chair   7 chairs
1 student   12 students
!! Books, chairs and students are **regular** plurals.

irregular plurals

'men' is an **irregular plural** :   1 man   2 **men**
'women' is an **irregular plural** :   1 woman   2 **women**
'people' is an **irregular plural** :   1 person   2 **people**

Q. What is the plural of man ?

Q. What is the plural of woman ?

Q. What is the plural of person ?

Q. How many men are there in this classroom ?

Q. How many women are there in this classroom ?

Q. How many people are there in this classroom ?

n. **family**   *n.* **mother**   *n.* **father**   *n.* **parents**

Q. What is your mother's name ?

Q. What is your father's name ?

Q. What are your parents' names ?

Q. Where is your family from ?

Q. How many people are there in your family ?

adj. **old**   *adj.* **young**   **How old ... ?**

Q. How old are you ?

Q. How old is your mother ?

Q. Is your father young ?
Q. How old is he ?

Q. Am I old ?

n. **boy**   *n.* **girl**

n. **child/children**   *n.* **adult**   *n.* **teenager**   *n.* **baby**

A **teenager** is a young person between thirteen and nineteen.

Children is an irregular plural.

Q.   What is the plural of child ?

Q.   Is a teenager a young person ?

Q.   Are there children in this room ?

Q.   Are we adults ?

Q.   Are you a baby ?

Q.   Are there children in your family ?

Q.   Are there babies in your family ?

Q.   How many boys and girls are there in your family ?

big numbers

100 = a hundred

135 = a hundred **and** thirty-five

1,000 = a thousand

5,372 = five thousand three hundred **and** seventy two

1,000,000 = a million

NB.   Not three ~~millions~~ (plural), but three **million**.

Q.   Say these numbers: 101   133   1200   1283

42,619   6,000,000   80,000,000

about

There are **about** 60 million people in Britain.

About four hundred students come to this school.

Q.   About how many students come to this school ?

Q.   About how many people are there in your country ?

Q.   About how old am I ?

Q.   About how old is he/she ?

Q. = **question**   *A.* = **answer**

Question : What colour is the board ?

Answer :   The board is white.

Question : Where is London ?

Answer :   London is in England.

_v._ **to ask**   **with**

We **ask** a question.

We **ask** questions **with** the words : what, where, which, who, how many, how old.

eg.   **What** is your name ?

        Where are you from ?

        How many students are there in the classroom ?

Q.   Ask (student's name) a question with the word 'what'.

Q.   Ask (student's name) a question with the word 'where'.

Q.   Ask (student's name) a question with the words 'how many'.

Q.   Ask (student's name) a question with the words 'how old'.

_v._ **to have**

I have

you have

he / she **has**

it **has**

we have

you have

they have

eg.   I **have** a pen.

        You **have** brown eyes.

        He **has** a bag.

        She **has** black hair.   **!!**   he/she/it **has**   NOT   ~~he/she/it have~~

---

questions with 'do'   (I, you, we, they)

We ask questions with the word 'do' (I, you, we, they)

Question : **Do** I have a pen ?

Answer :   Yes, I have a pen

Q.   **Do** I have a book ?

Q.   **Do** you have an umbrella ?

Q.   **Do** we have pens ?

Q.   **Do** they have bags ?

Q.   Do I have a book ?

A.   Yes, you have a book.

Q.   Do you have a pen ?

A.   Yes, I have a pen.

Q.   Do we have chairs ?

A.   Yes, we have chairs.

Q.   Do they have bags ?

A.   Yes, they have bags.

Q. Do I have ... hair ?*

Q. Do I have ... eyes ?*

Q. Do you have black or brown hair ?*

Q. Do you have blue or brown eyes ?*

Q. Do they have brown/blue/green eyes ?*

adj. **long**   *adj.* **short**

Q. What is the opposite of long ?

Q. Do I have long or short hair ?

Q. Do you have long or short hair ?

---

questions with 'does'   (he, she, it)

We ask questions with the word 'does' (he, she, it)

Question : **Does** he have a pen ?   NOT ~~Do he have a pen~~ ?
Answer :   Yes, he **has** a pen.   NOT ~~Yes, he have a pen.~~

Q.   **Does** she have long hair ?
Q.   **Does** the classroom have four walls ?

Q. Does he have a pen ?
A. Yes, he has a pen.

Q. Does she have a bag ?
A. Yes, she has a bag.

Q. Does he/she have a book ?

Q. Does the classroom have four walls ?

Q. Does he/she have long or short hair ?

Q. Does he/she have brown/blue/green eyes ?*

Q. Does he/she have black/brown/blond hair ?*

Q. What colour hair does he/she have ?

Q. What colour eyes does he/she have ?

---

negative answers

We say negative answers with 'do not' (I , you, we, they)
Q.   Do I/you/we/they have black hair ?
+A.   Yes I/we/you/they have black hair.
-A.   No I/you/we/they **do not** have black hair.

> **We say negative answers with 'does not'** (he, she, it)
> Q.   Does he/she have black hair ?
> +A.   Yes he/she has black hair.   NOT ~~Yes he have~~ ...
> -A.   No he/she **does not** have black hair. NOT ~~No he does not has~~ ...

Q.   Do I have a bag ?

Q.   Do I have an umbrella ?

Q.   Do you have blue/brown eyes ?*

Q.   Do you have long/short hair ?*

Q.   Does he/she have blue/brown eyes ?*

Q.   Does he/she have black/brown hair ?*

Q.   Does he/she have long/short hair ?*

Q.   Does the classroom have red walls ?

Q.   Do we have yellow chairs ?

Q.   Do they have umbrellas ?

> *n.* **house**   *n.* **garden**
> *n.* **flat**   *n.* **swimming pool**

Q.   Do you have a house or a flat in your country ?

Q.   Does your house/flat have a garden ?

Q.   Is there a swimming pool in your city ?

> *n.* **home**   *n.* **school**
> **at home** = in your house   **at school** = in the school

Q.   Are you at home ?
A.   No, I am not at home, but I am at school.

Q.   Do you have pictures at home ?

Q.   Do you have a swimming pool at home ?

Q.   Do you have a garden at home ?

> *n.* **computer**   *n.* **car**   *n.* **telephone**   *n.* **television**

Q.   Is there a television in the classroom ?
Q.   Do you have a television at home ?

Q.   Is there a computer in the classroom ?
Q.   Do have a computer at home ?

Q. Do you have a car ?

Q. Do you have a telephone ?
Q. Where is it ?*

Q. Do you have a telephone in your bag ?

n. **sister**   *n.* **brother**

Q. Do you have brothers and sisters ?
Q. How many do you have ?

Q. What is your brother's name ?
Q. What colour hair does he have ?
Q. What colour eyes does he have ?

Q. What is your sister's name ?
Q. What colour hair does she have ?
Q. What colour eyes does she have ?

exercise

1. I am from ....

2. He is .... Italy.

3. Brazil is a .... country.

4. London is a .... city.

5. The opposite of hot is ....

6. The opposite of .... is dirty.

7. The five vowels are ....., ... , ..., ..., ...

8. The days of the week are ...., ..., ...,

............................., ..., ..., ...

9. Today is ....

10. B is .... A and C.

11. Monday is .... Tuesday.

12. .... is after Tuesday.

exercise
1. He is .... man.
2. It is .... umbrella.
3. .... mouse is .... animal.
4. .... elephant is .... big animal.
5. My shirt .... white.

6. His jeans .... blue.

7. **Q.** .... you have a book ?

   A. Yes, I .... a book.

8. **Q.** .... she have a bag ?

   A. Yes, she .... a bag.

9. **Q.** .... they have umbrellas ?

   A. No, they .... have umbrellas.

10. **Q.** .... she have a telephone in her bag ?

    A. No, she .... not .... a telephone in her bag.

exercise
Answer with a sentence.

1. Where are you from ?

   .... I'm from Korea ....

2. What is the opposite of black ?

   ....

3. Which day is before Saturday ?

   ....

4. Which day is after Tuesday ?

   ....

5. Do you have a car ?

   ....

6. Does your mother have a computer ?

   ....

Unit 3

n. **job**

n. **teacher**   *n.* **policeman**

n. **doctor**   *n.* **dentist**

n. **taxi driver**   *n.* **secretary**

eg.   I have a **job**. I am a **teacher**.

My mother has a **job**. She is a **doctor**.

Q. Do I have a job ?
A. Yes, you have a job.

Q. What is my job ?
A. You are a teacher.

Q. Does your mother have a job ?
A. What is her job ?

Q. Do you have a job ?
Q. What is your job ?
A. I am a ...

Q. Does he/she have a job ? - Ask.
Q. What is his job ? - Ask.

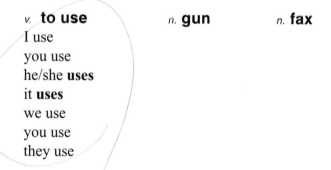

v. **to use**   *n.* **gun**   *n.* **fax**

I use
you use
he/she **uses**
it **uses**
we use
you use
they use

eg.   I am a teacher. I **use** a pen, a book and a board in the classroom.

My mother is a secretary . She **uses** a computer, a telephone and a **fax** in her job.

My father is a policeman. He **uses** a **gun** in his job.

Q. What do I use in the classroom ?

Q. What does a secretary use in her job ?

Q. Does a policeman use a gun in his job ?

Q. Does a doctor use a gun in his/her job ?

Q. Do we use a computer in the classroom ?

Q. What does a taxi driver use in his job ?

Q. What do you use in the classroom ?

!! We **use** 'do' in questions with I, you, we, they.
We **use** 'do not' in negative answers with I, you, we, they.
We **use** 'does' in questions with he, she, it.
We **use** 'does not' in negative answers with he, she, it.

Q. Who uses a gun in his/her job ?

Q. Who uses the board in the classroom ?

Q. Who is from (a country) in the classroom ?*

n. **bed**   *n.* **bath**   *n.* **room**
n. **bedroom**   *n.* **bathroom**   *n.* **living room**

Q. Do you have a house or a flat ?
Q. How many rooms are there in your house/flat ?

Q. Is there a bed in the classroom ?
Q. Do you have a bed in your bedroom ?

Q. Is there a bath in the classroom ?
Q. Do you have a bath in your bathroom ?

Q. Do you have a living room in your house/flat ?

Q. Where is the television in your house/flat ?

v. **to like**
I like
you like
he/she likes
we like
you like
they like

Q. Do you like your house/flat ?

Q. Do you like a clean bed?

Q. Do you like a dirty bathroom ?

Q. Do you like my shirt/trousers/jumper ?

Q. Do you like the chairs in your living room ?

n. **tea**   *n.*   **coffee**   *n.* **milk**

Q. What colour is milk ?

Q. Do you like tea ?

Q. Do you like coffee ?

with   without   n. sugar

white coffee = coffee **with** milk
black coffee = coffee **without** milk

Q. What is white coffee ?
A. White coffee is coffee with milk.

Q. What is black coffee ?
A. Black coffee is coffee without milk.

Q. Do you like black coffee ?

Q. Do you like tea/coffee with or without sugar ?

v. **to prefer**

I like coffee but I **prefer** tea.
I like cats but I **prefer** dogs.

Q. Do you prefer cats or dogs ?

Q. Do you prefer tea or coffee ?

Q. Do you prefer my shirt or your shirt ?

v. **to eat**   *v.* **to drink**
n. **food**   *n.* **water**
n. **bread**   *n.* **wine**
n. **rice**

Q. What colour is wine ?

Q. Do you like wine ?

Q. Do you eat rice ?

Q. Do you drink wine ?
Q. Which do you prefer, red wine or white wine ?

Q. Do you eat bread ?
Q. Which do you prefer, white bread or brown bread ?

adj. **good**   *adj.* **bad**

Q. Are you a good student ?

Q. Do you have good wine in your country ?

Q. Is it a good picture or a bad picture ?*

v. **to think**

I **think** it is a good picture. (teacher points)
Question :   What do you **think** ?
Positive answer :   I **think** it is a good picture.
Negative answer :   I **do not think** it is a good picture.

Q.   I think English food is good. - What do you think ?

Q.   I don't think England is a cold country ? - What do you think ?

Q.   Do you think it is a good picture ?*
Q.   What do you think ?*

Q.   Do you think he/she is a good student ?

very   **quite**
An elephant is a **very** big animal.
England is **quite** cold.

Q.   Is an elephant a very big animal ?

Q.   Do you think a mouse is a very small animal ?

Q.   Do you think it is hot or cold today ?
Q.   Quite hot/cold or very hot/cold ?

Q.   Do you think it is a good picture ?
Q.   Quite good/bad or very good/bad ?

Q.   Do you think London is quite big or very big ?

Q.   Do you think your country is big or small ?
Q.   Quite big/small or very big/small ?

n. **flag***

Q.   Does your country have a flag ?
Q.   What colour is it ?

Q.   What colour is this flag ?
A.   That flag is blue and white.

Q.   Is the flag of your country in this picture ?
Q.   Which flag is it ?

n. **country**	*n.* **nationality**	*n.* **language**
England	British	English
America	American	English
Brazil	Brazilian	Portuguese
Japan	Japanese	Japanese
Korea	Korean	Korean
Poland	Polish	Polish
Colombia	Colombian	Spanish
Italy	Italian	Italian
China	Chinese	Chinese

v. **to speak**

I **speak** English.
He **speaks** French.
An **English person speaks** English.
A **Colombian person speaks** Spanish.

Q. What language do I speak ?

Q. What language do you speak ?

Q. What language does a Polish person speak ?

Q. What language does a Spanish person speak ?

Q. Does a French person speak Japanese ?

Q. Do you speak French ?

Q. What language does he/she speak ? - Ask.

so

eg.   I don't like milk, **so** I prefer black coffee.
I am from England, **so** I am British and I speak English.
He is from Colombia, **so** he is Colombian and he speaks Spanish.

Q. Where are you from ?
A. I am ...
Q. So, what nationality are you and what language do you speak ?
A. I am ... and I speak ...

Q. Where is he/she from ?
A. He / she is from ...
Q. So, what nationality is he/she and what language does he/she speak ?
A. He/she is ... and he/she speaks ...

n. **home** = your house/flat   **at home** = in your house
at school = in the school/classroom

Q. Are you at home ?
Q. So, where are you ?

Q. Do you speak English at home ?
Q. So, what language do you speak at home ?

v. **to go** (there)   *v.* **to come** (here)

eg.   We **come** here to speak English.
We **go** home after school.
He **comes** here on Mondays.
He does **not come** here on Saturdays.

!!   We say he **goes**, she **goes**, it **goes**.

Q. Do you come here on Mondays ?

Q. Do you come here on Sundays ?

Q. Do you go home after school ?

Q. Where do you go after school ?

> *n.* **breakfast**   *n.* **morning**   **When ... ?**
> *n.* **lunch**   *n.* **afternoon**
> *n.* **dinner**   *n.* **evening**
>
> eg.   We have breakfast **in** the morning.
>   We have lunch **in** the afternoon.
>   We have dinner **in** the evening.
>
> *!!*   We **have** breakfast, lunch and dinner.

Q. When do you have breakfast ?

Q. When do you have lunch ?

Q. When do you have dinner ?

Q. Do you have breakfast at home ?
Q. Do you eat dinner there ?

Q. Do you come here in the morning or the afternoon ?

Q. Does he/she have breakfast/lunch before he/she comes here ? - Ask.

> *adv.* **always** = 100 %
> *adv.* **never** = 0%
> *adv.* **ever** - We use **ever** in questions.
> Q.   Do you **ever** have breakfast in the evening ?
> A.   No, I **never** have breakfast in the evening, but I **always** have breakfast in the morning.

Q. Do you ever have breakfast in the evening ?
A. No, I never have breakfast in the evening.

Q. Do you ever have lunch in the afternoon ?
A. Yes, I always have lunch in the afternoon.

Q. Do you ever come to school on Saturdays ?

Q. Do you ever speak English in the classroom ?

Q. Do you ever use a computer in the classroom ?

Q. Do you ever have lunch in the classroom ?

> *adv.* **sometimes** = 10 - 50 %   *n.* **restaurant**
> *adv.* **usually** = 80%
> I **usually** have dinner at home, but **sometimes** I have dinner in a restaurant.
> I don't **always** drink tea for breakfast. I **usually** drink tea, but I **sometimes** drink coffee.

Q. Do you usually have dinner at home or in a restaurant?
Q. Do you always have dinner at home ?
A. No, I do not always have dinner at home, but sometimes I have dinner in a restaurant.

Q. What do you usually drink with your breakfast ? *[handwritten: I usuall drink coff with]*

Q. Do you always drink ... with your breakfast ?

Q. What language do you usually speak at home ? *[handwritten: I usually speak Korean at home?]*

Q. Do you always speak ... at home ?

Use **always**, **usually**, **sometimes** or **never** in your answers.

Q. Do you ever come to school on Mondays ? *[handwritten: I always come to school on Mondays?]*

Q. Do you ever speak your language at home ? *[handwritten: I s]*

Q. Do you ever drink wine with your dinner ?

Q. Do you ever eat lunch here in the school ?

Q. Does the teacher ever speak your language in the classroom ? *[handwritten: No The]*

Q. Do you ever eat dinner in a restaurant ?

Q. Does he/she ever use a computer at home ? - Ask. *[handwritten: yes]*

Q. Does he/she ever eat rice for breakfast ? - Ask. *[handwritten: yes]*

Q. Does he/she ever use a gun ? - Ask.

n. **music**

rock	heavy metal	classical
pop	jazz	opera

[handwritten: Favourite / Like / quite Like / don't Like]

adj. **favourite**   **kind(s) of**

eg.   Dogs, cats, elephants and mice are **kinds of** animals.
         I quite like cats and dogs, but my **favourite** animals are elephants.

eg.   Rock, pop and classical are **kinds of** music.
         I quite like jazz and classical, but my **favourite** music is pop.

Q. What kinds of animals do you like ?

Q. What is your favourite animal ?

Q. What kinds of music do you like ?

Q. What is your favourite music ?

Q. What is your favourite kind of car ?

Q. What is his/her favourite colour ? - Ask.

v. **to listen (to)**   *n.* **radio**

eg.   I **listen to** music on the **radio**.
         I **listen to** music in my car.

Q. Do you have a radio ?

Q. Do you ever listen to music on the radio ?

Q. What kind of music do you usually listen to ?

Q. Do you ever listen to heavy metal ?

Q. Do you ever listen to classical music ?

Q. Does he/she ever listen to pop music ? - Ask*

exercise
What kind of music do we listen to ?

	teacher	student
usually (favourite)	dance music.	pop
sometimes	classical, ~~blues~~ classical	
sometimes	blues.	rok
never	Country +western	heavy metal.

poison

v. **to watch**   *n.* **television**   *n.* **film**
                                                         n. **sport**
                                                         n. **the news**

eg.   I **usually** watch television **in the evening.**
      We watch the news **on** television.

Q. Do you have a television ?

Q. Do you ever watch sport on television ?
Q. What kind of sport ?

Q. Do you ever watch films on television ?

Q. Do you ever watch the news on television ?

Q. What is his/her favourite film ? - Ask.

Q. Does he/she like sport ? - Ask.
Q. What is his/her favourite sport ? - Ask.

v. **to understand**

Q. Do you understand English radio ?

Q. Do you understand English television ?   I don't understand

Q. Do you understand the news in English ?   I somtimes und   3.

Q. Do you always understand me ?   1 always understand youz   2.29

Q. Do you think men understand women ?
Q. Do you think women understand men ?

Q. Do you ever listen to English music ?
Q. When you listen to English music, do you always understand the words ?

2 som elne und dae word

adj. **easy**	adj. **difficult**	n. **lesson**
2+2 = ?	This question is **easy**.	This is an English **lesson**.
447x375 = ?	This question is **difficult**.	

Q. Do you think it is easy to understand ~~your~~ *my* language ?

Q. Do you think it is easy to understand English ?

I don't think it is easy ~

Q. Do you always come to the lesson ?

P. I always come to th ~

Q. Do you think this lesson is quite easy ?

yes. I.

Q. Is it easy to use a telephone ?

yes, is it

Q. Is it difficult to use a computer ?

Q. Do you think my job is easy or difficult ?
Q. Very easy/difficult or quite easy/difficult ?

the same (as)   adj. **different**

eg.   English and American people are **different**, but they speak **the same** language.
      I don't speak **the same** language **as** you but I speak a **different** language.

Q. Is your flag the same as the British flag ?   *No my flag different to the British.*

Q. Is your language the same as English ?   *No we don.*

Q. Do we speak the same language ?   *No we don't speak*

Q. Is this chair the same colour as that chair ?   *that chair*

Q. Is classical music the same as pop music ?   *No*

Q. Do you always have the same thing for breakfast ?   *I * Somtim have the same thing for breakfast.*

adv. **generally** = usually

Q. What language do you generally speak at home ?
A. I generally speak ... *Korean at home*

Q. What language do you speak at this school ?   *I*

Q. What do you generally have for breakfast ?   *I generally*

Q. What kind of music do you generally listen to ?

n.   **noun**

The word elephant is a **noun**.
The word table is a **noun**.   *!!*   We use **nouns** for things.
The word people is a plural **noun**.

Q. Is the word mouse a noun ?

Q. Is the word cat a noun ?
Q. Is it a singular or plural noun ?

Q. Is the word chairs a noun ?

Q. Is it a singular or plural noun ?

n. **action**
To listen is an **action**.
To eat is an **action**.
To drink is an **action**.

Q. Is to eat an action ?

Q. Is to listen an action ?

Q. Is to drink an action ? *Yes to drink is an action*

Q. Is to speak an action ?

n. **verb**   *!!* We use **verbs** for actions.

Q. Is to listen a verb ?

Q. Is to eat a verb ?

Q. Is the word elephant a verb ?

Q. So, what is it ?

I watch television.   to watch = **verb**
                        television = **noun**

I listen to music.   to listen = **verb**
                        music = **noun**

Q. What is the verb in these sentences ?

I come to school.
I use a book at school.
This flag is red, white and blue.
You are a student.

n. **adjective**
The words **big** and **small**, **clean** and **dirty**, **hot** and **cold** are **adjectives**.
!! We usually use adjectives before nouns.
eg.   Scotland is a **cold** country.
       He has a **big** dog.

Q. Is the word big an adjective ?

Q. Is the word hot an adjective ?

Q. Is the word red an adjective ?

Q. Is the word gun an adjective ?

Q. Is the word listen an adjective ?

Q. What are the adjectives in these sentences ?
  a. Brazil is a big, hot country.
  b. My shoes are clean.
  c. An elephant is a big animal.

  She likes brown sugar in her coffee.

Q. What is the verb in this sentence ?

Q. What are the two nouns in this sentence ?

Q. What is the adjective in this sentence ?

exercise

Which of these words are adjectives, verbs or nouns ?

be	flag	like	horrible	have
Tuesday	easy	blue	think	understand
girl	dirty	alphabet	policeman	different

adjective	verb	noun
....	....	....
....	....	....
....	....	....
....	....	....
....	....	....

Unit 4

v. **to teach**   *v.* **to study**

Q.   Do you teach English ? ⁿ

Q.   Do I study English ?

Q.   What language does he/she study ?

Q.   Do you ever study English at home ?

---

present continuous
We use the **present continuous** for an action we are doing **now**.
eg.   I **am teaching**. (now)
       You **are studying**. (now)

present continuous of the verb **to listen**

subject	to be	verb + ing
I	am	listening
you	are	listening
he/she	is	listening
we	are	listening
you	are	listening
they	are	listening

Q.   **Are** you **listening** to **me** ?
+A.   Yes, I **am listening** to you.
Q.   **Are** you **watching** television ?
-A.   No, I **am** <u>not</u> **watching** television.

Q.   Are you speaking English ?
A.   Yes, I am speaking English.

Q.   Are you speaking (student's language) ?
A.   No, I am not speaking ...

Q.   Are you studying English ?
A.   Yes, I am studying English.

Q.   Am I speaking English ?
A.   Yes, you are speaking English.

Q.   Are you listening to me ?
A.   Yes, I am listening to you.

Q.   Are you watching television ?
A.   No, I am not watching television.

v. **to sit**   *v.* **to stand**

Q. Are you sitting or standing ?

Q. Am I sitting or standing ?

Q. Where are you sitting ?

Q. Who is sitting between (student name) and (student name) ?

present simple and present continuous

The **present simple** and the **present continuous** are **different**.
We use the **present simple** for an action we do **generally**.
eg.   I drink tea in the morning.
We use the **present continuous** for an action we are doing **now**.
eg.   I am sitting on the chair.
          I am not using a computer now, *but* I use a computer at home.
          I am not watching television now, *but* I usually watch television in the evening.

Q. Are you listening to the radio ?
Q. Do you ever listen to the radio ?

Q. Are you watching TV ?
Q. Do you ever watch TV in the evenings ?

Q. Are you drinking coffee ?
Q. Do you drink coffee for breakfast ?

Q. Is he using a computer ?
Q. What does he use in the classroom ?

Q. Are you speaking (student's language) ?
Q. Do you speak (student's language) ?

Q.   Listen to these sentences - are they '**simple**' or '**continuous**'
          I am speaking to you.   c
          I speak English.   s
          I watch television in the evening.   s
          They are listening to me.   C
          I am eating bread.   c
          I eat breakfast in the morning.   s

Q. When do we use the present simple ?
A. We use the present simple for an action we do generally.

Q. Say a sentence in the present simple.

Q. When do we use the present continuous ?
A. We use the present continuous for an action we are doing now.

Q. Say a sentence in the present continuous.

adj. **right**   adj. **wrong**

There is five chairs. - **wrong** *are*
There are five chairs. - **right**

brekfist - **wrong** spelling
breakfast - **right** spelling

I am speak English. - **wrong**
I am speaking English. - **right**

Q.   Listen to these sentences : are they **right** or **wrong ?**

The plural of person is persons.

The plural of person is people. √

A is after B.

C is after B. √

I am speak English.

I am speaking English. √

I am sit on a chair.

I am sitting on a chair. √

Q.   Is this the right spelling ?*
       i. Wensday   ii. wich   iii. brakefast   iv. vegetable   v. ciling
                                                                              ceiling

Q.   London is in England. Am I right ?

Q.   Paris is in Germany. Am I right ?

Q.   Where is Tokyo ?
Q.   Is he/she right ?

why ?   **because**
We use **why** in questions and **because** in answers.
Question :   **Why** do you drink black coffee ?
Answer :   **Because** I don't like milk.

Q.   Why are you here ?
A.   Because I am studying English.

       The plural of man is mans.
Q.   Is that right ?
Q.   Why is it wrong ?
A.   Because the plural of man ...

       I am teach English ?
Q.   Is that right ?
Q.   Why is it wrong ?
A.   Because we say ...

kinds of food

n. **fruit**	n. **vegetables**	n. **meat**	n. **fish**
n. **apple**	n. **potato**	n. **beef**	
n. **orange**	n. **carrot**	n. **chicken**	
n. **drink**	n. **tomato**		
n. **banana**	n. **lettuce**		
n. **beer**			

mushrooms

a lot of   **not a lot of**

English people drink **a lot of** beer.
Japanese people eat **a lot of** rice.
I eat **a lot of** carrots because they are my favourite vegetables.
I **don't eat a lo**t of fish because I don't like it.

Q.   Do you eat meat ?

Q.   Do you prefer chicken or beef ?

Q.   What is your favourite drink ?
Q.   Do you drink a lot of it ?

Q.   What is your favourite fruit ?
Q.   Do you eat a lot of it ?

Q.   What colour are :
   a. carrots   b. tomatoes   c. lemons

Q.   Are apples always the same colour ?

Q.   Do you have a lot of books at home ?
Q.   About how many ?

Q.   Are there a lot of cinemas in this city ?   *There*

   v. **to read**
   n. **newspaper**   n. **magazine**

Q.   Do you read a newspaper ?
Q.   Which newspaper do you usually read ?

Q.   Do you ever read English newpapers ?

Q.   Do you understand English newspapers ?

Q.   Do you read magazines ?
Q.   What kind of magazines ? (sport,fashion, music, car)

Q.   Do you ever read in bed ?

v. **to write** (to)
n. **letter**   n. **postcard**   n. **friend**

Q.   Do you have a lot of friends in this city ?

Q.   Do you ever go to the cinema/pub with your friends ?

Q.   Who writes on the board ?

Q.   Do you ever write letters in English ?

Q.   Do you ever write postcards to your friends ?

Q.   Do your friends ever write letters to you ?

chewing gum.

v. **to live** (in)
I am **from** Scotland but I **live** in London.

Q.   Do you live in a house or a flat ?

Q.   Where does he/she live ? - Ask!

Q.   Who lives in the White House ?

Q.   **Which month is it now ?**

Q.   **What is your first name ?**

Q.   **Are you studying English ?**
Q.   **Do you ever study at home ?**

Q.   **Do you eat a lot of fish ?**   청속시 .

Q.   **What do you usually drink when you go to the pub ?**

---

v. **to put**
n. **key**   n. **money**   n. **pocket**   n. **wallet**
I am **putting** my pen on the table.
I am **putting** my money in my pocket.
your · your.

to pick someting up

Q   What am I doing ? - (pen on table)   *I*   *wi you are putting*

Q.   What am I doing ? - (thing in pocket)

Q.   Put your book on the floor.
Q.   What is he/she doing ?

Q.   What do you have in your pocket ?

Q.   Where do you put your money ?

Q.   How many keys do you have ?

Q. What do you put in your bag before you come to school ? *I put in.*

Q. Do you put a lot of sugar in your coffee ?

Q. What do you put :
  a. on a plate   b. on your cereal   c. in your fridge ?

freezer   *almost*
nearly

n. **envelope**   *n.* **stamp**   *n.* **post box***   *n.* **paper**
We write a letter on **paper**.
We put the letter in an **envelope**.
We put a **stamp** on the envelope.

Q. Do you write a lot of letters ?
Q. Who do you write to ?   *I write to* ~ .

Q. Do you always use white paper ?   *Yes*

Q. What do we put on an envelope ?   *w*

Q. Where do we put letters and postcards ?

in post box

Q. What colour are the post boxes in your country ?

adv. **a lot**   *adv.* **not a lot**
We use **a lot** of before a noun.
We use **a lot** without a noun.
eg.   I write **a lot of** letters.
    I read **a lot.**

Q. Do you read a lot ?

Q. Do you sleep a lot ?

Q. Do you study a lot ?

Q. Do you go to the cinema a lot ?

v. **to call**   *n.* **phone number**   *n.* **code**
We write : <u>0171</u> <u>379 1998</u>
        code   number
We say : O*-one-seven-one   three-seven-nine   one-<u>double nine</u>-eight
*We do not say 'zero' for telephone numbers in English, but we use the letter '**O**'.

Q. What is your telephone number ?

Q. What is the code for your city/country ?

Q. What is the telephone number of this school ?

Q. Do you call your parents a lot ?

Q. Do you usually call your friends in the evening ?

Q. What number do you call for the police in your country ?
Q. In this country ?

v. **to give**

I am **giving** you my book.*

or

I am **giving** my book **to** you.

Q.   What am I doing ?

A.   You are giving me your book.

Q.   Do your mother and father ever give you money ?

Q.   Who do you give your telephone number to ?

n. **example** (of)

An apple is an **example** of a fruit.

Small is an **example** of an adjective.

Q.   Give **me** an **example** of an animal ?

A.   A dog (is an example of an animal).

Q.   Give me an example of :

a. a fruit   b. a vegetable   c. a colour.

Q.   Give me an example of :

a. a verb   b. a noun   c. an adjective.

Q.   Give me an example of a good job.

Q.   Give me an example of the present simple.

Q.   Give me an example of the present continuous.

for example   eg.

I like a lot of vegetables; **for example**, carrots, potatoes and tomatoes.

Plural nouns are sometimes irregular, **eg**. men, children and mice.

v. **to know**

I **know** your name, but I **don't know** your address.

Q.   Do you know my name ?

Q.   Do you know the alphabet ?

Q.   Say it.

Q.   Do you know the spelling of breakfast ?

Q.   What is it ?

Q.   Do you know the plural of that ?

Q.   What is it ?

Q.   Do you know your telephone number ?

Q.   Do you know my telephone number ?

Q.   Do you know the address of this school ?

Q.   What is it ?

Q.   Do you give your telephone number to people you don't know ?

n. **gerund** (1)
The **gerund** is a verb + ing
eg.   do**ing**, hav**ing**, ask**ing**, us**ing**, eat**ing**, drink**ing**, be**ing**

We sometimes use the gerund after verbs.

v. **to like** + gerund   *v.* **to prefer** + gerund
We use the **gerund** after the verb 'to like' and the verb 'to prefer'.
eg.   I like drink**ing** wine but I prefer drink**ing** beer.
       I don't like watch**ing** television in the morning. I prefer listen**ing** to the radio.

!! These sentences are NOT present continuous but they are present simple + gerund.

Q.   Do you like reading letters from your friends ?

Q.   Do you prefer reading or writing letters ?

Q.   Do you read magazines a lot ?
Q.   What magazines do you like reading ?

Q.   Do you prefer studying or watching television ?

Q.   Do you like going to the cinema with your friends ?

Q.   What do you like doing on Sundays ?

Q.   Docs he/she like studying English ? - Ask.

v. **to sing**   *v.* **to dance** (to music)
n. **song**

Q.   Do you like dancing ?

Q.   What kind of music do you like dancing to ?

Q.   Do you like singing ?

Q.   Do you ever sing in the bath ?

Q.   What is your favourite song at the moment ?

Q.   Do you ever dance in the evening ?

adv. **often**
eg.   I **often** go to the cinema.
       I **usually** go to the cinema on Saturday afternoons.

Q.   Do you often go to the cinema ?

Q.   Do you often go to the pub after school ?
Q.   What do you usually drink ?

Q. Do you often drink wine with your dinner ?

Q. Do you usually drink red or white wine ?

Q. Are you often at home in the evening ?

Q. What do you usually do ?

Q. Do you prefer reading newspapers or magazines ?

Q. What are the two opposites of the word 'right' ?

Q. Give me an example of a big/small animal.

Q. Do you usually call your parents or write to them ?

Q. Do you sit down or stand up when you:
  a. have a bath ?   b. have a shower ?

when

Unit 5

v. **to sleep**   *v.* **to work**   *n.* **work**

Q. Are you sleeping ?

Q. Do you sleep a lot ?

Q. Do you like working ?
Q. Are you at work now ?

Q. Do you have a job ?
Q. Where do you work ?

Q. Do you ever sleep on the floor ?
Q. Where do you sleep ?

How long?   **for**
Q.   **How long** do you study **for** ?
A.   I study **for** 3 hours.

Q. How long do you usually sleep for ?

Q. How long do you think I work for ?

Q. How long do you generally watch television for in the evening ?

Q. Do you ever read in bed ?
Q. How long for ?

n. **day**   *n.* **night**
   during   **at**
We usually work **during** the day and sleep **at night**.
You study English **during** the lesson.

Q. Do you ever work at night ?

Q. What kind of people work at night ?

Q. What do you usually do during the day ?

Q. What do you do during the lesson ?

Q. Do you ever sleep during the lesson ?

Q. How long do you study for a day ?

Q. What does the teacher do during the lesson ?

Q.   **Do you know the colours of the Spanish Flag ?**

Q.   **Do you know how many people live in your city/country ?**

Q.   **Who works at this school ?**

Q.   **Does he / she ever sleep in the classroom ?**

Q.   **What do you like doing in the evening ?**

v. **to cook**   *n.* **cook**

oxtail soup

Q.   Do you like cooking ?

Q.   Are you a good cook ?

Q.   What kind of food do you like cooking ?

Q.   What kind of food is easy to cook ?

Q.   Do you cook a lot at home ?

n. **soup**   *n.* **pasta**   *n.* **eggs**

Q.   How long do you cook pasta ?

A.   I cook pasta for about ...

Q.   And rice ?

Q.   How long do you cook eggs ?

Q.   Which do you prefer, pasta or rice ?

Q.   Do you ever eat soup for breakfast ?

I thing so

Q.   What kinds of soup do you know ?

Q.   What kind of soup do you prefer ?

countable and uncountable nouns

adj. **countable**   *adj.* **uncountable**

A lot of nouns are **countable** in English.
Book is a **countable** noun - we say one book, five books, ten books ...
Pen is a **countable** noun - we say one pen, five pens, ten pens ...

Q.   Is 'chair' a countable noun ?

Q.   Is 'person' a countable noun ?

But a lot of nouns are **uncountable**.
Water is an **uncountable** noun - we don't say one water, five water ...
Rice is an **uncountable** noun - we don't say one rice, five rice ...

Different kinds of food and drink are usually uncountable.
pasta   rice   milk

a loaf of bread
a slice of bread.

Q. Is 'water' an uncountable noun ?

Q. Is 'bread' a countable noun ?

Q. Is 'milk' countable or uncountable ?

Q. Are these nouns countable or uncountable ?

food	pasta	banana	rice	colour	meat	house
hair	news	hour	milk	wine	beer	lunch
evening	soap	soup	money*	pound	dollar	envelope

Knives

n. **spoon**   n. **knife*** and **fork**   n. **chopsticks**

Q. Do you use a knife and fork or chopsticks in your country ?

Q. Is it easy for you to use chopsticks ?

Q. What kind of food do we eat with a spoon ?

Q. In which countries do people use chopsticks ?

n. **kitchen**   n. **microwave**   n. **cooker**

Q. Do you have a big kitchen ?

Q. Do you have a cooker in your kitchen ?

Q. Do you ever use a microwave ?
Q. What kind of food do you cook in a microwave ?

Q. Do you prefer cooking with a microwave or a cooker ?

v. **to keep**   n. **fridge**   n. **freezer**   n. **ice-cream**

We **keep** milk, meat and eggs in the fridge.
We **keep** ice-cream in the freezer.

Q. What do we keep in the fridge ?

Q. Where do we keep ice-cream ?

Q. Do you keep milk in the freezer ?
Q. So, where do you keep it ?

Q. Where do you keep your :
a. keys ?   b. money ? c. wallet ?

Q. Where do you keep addresses and telephone numbers ?

n. **cup** (of)   n. **glass** (of)   n. **bottle** (of)

Q. Do you use a cup or a glass for :
a. wine   b. coffee   c. beer   d. milk ?

a prece of pasta
a grain of rice   *a portion of rice.*

Q. Do you ever drink a glass of wine with your dinner ?
Q. Do you ever drink a bottle of wine ?

Q. What do you usually drink for breakfast ?
Q. How many cups/glasses of ... do you drink ?

Q. Do you prefer drinking beer from a bottle or a glass ?

n. **plate** (of)   n. **bowl** (of)

Q. Do you eat soup from a plate ?

Q. Do you ever have a bowl of soup for lunch ?

Q. Do you usually eat from a bowl or a plate ?

Q. What do people eat from a bowl ?

n. **cupboard**   n. **drawer**
n. **clothes**   n. **wardrobe**
We keep cups, plates and bowls in a **cupboard**.
We keep knives, forks and spoons in a **drawer**.
We keep clothes in a **wardrobe**.

Q. Where do you keep your plates, bowls and cups ?

Q. Where do you keep your knives and forks ?

Q. What kind of clothes do we keep in a wardrobe ? *we keep ___ in a wardrobe*

Q. What kind of clothes do we keep in a drawer ?

v. **to boil**   n. **kettle**   n. **saucepan**
We use a **kettle** to **boil** water.
We use a **saucepan** to cook food.

Q. What do we use to boil water ? *We u*

Q. Do you use a kettle to boil water in your country ?

Q. How do you cook pasta ?

You boil Pasta in water
= You cook Pasta by boiling it in water.

v. **to wash**   v. **do the washing** = wash your clothes
n. **sink**   v. **do the washing-up** = wash your plates, bowls and cups

Q. Do you wash your face in the morning ?

Q. What do you use when you wash ? *I to I use a soap to wash when.*

Q. What do you do when your clothes are dirty ? *I do the washing when my clothes are di*

Q. What do you do when your plates are dirty ? *I do " when*

Q. Where do you do the washing up ? *I do the washing up in a sink*

© Avalon Book Company Ltd., 1999

[handwritten: Adj + Noun.]
[handwritten: verb + Adverb.]

regular adverbs

adjective		adverb	
adj.	bad	adv.	**badly**
adj.	**quick**	adv.	**quickly**
adj.	**slow**	adv.	**slowly**

We usually use adjectives before a noun.
eg.   I like a **quick** drink after work.
We usually use adverbs after a verb.
eg.   The teacher speaks **quickly**.

Q. What do you eat when you have a quick lunch ?   *[handwritten: I eat sandwich. when I have a ~.]*

Q. Do you like dancing to slow music ?

Q. Do you usually speak your language slowly ?

Q. Does a microwave cook food quickly ?   *[handwritten: yes 1]*

irregular adverbs

adjective	adverb
good	**well**

eg.   He speaks English **well**.

Q. Do you speak English well ?

Q. Do you think a microwave cooks food well ?

Q. Do you know him ?
Q. Do you know him/her well ?

Q. Do you know this city well ?

Q. Do you always sleep well ?

v. **can**
You **can** speak your language well.
I **can** use a computer.

negative = **cannot / can't***
I **can't** speak your language well.
My mother **can't** use a computer.

The verb **can** is *irregular* - we do not use an 's' for he, she or it.
eg.   He **can** speak 3 different languages.
        She **can** sing very well.

Q. Can you stand on your chair ?   *[handwritten: yes I can stand on my chair of]*
Q. Can you stand on the ceiling ?

Q. Can we eat soup with a fork ?

Q. Can you use a computer ?

[handwritten: can't pronunciation = carnt]

Q. How many languages can you speak ?

Q. Can you speak English quickly ?

Q. Do you like singing ?
Q. Can you sing well ?   ~~I cool~~ *I can't*

Q. Give me an example of a person who can sing very well.

Q. Ask a question with can.

Q. Can you always understand my questions ?

Q. How long can we keep :
 a. milk in the fridge ?   b. fruit in a bowl ?   *we can we keep.*

> *v.* **to play**   *n.* **sport**   *n.* **game**
> *n.* **football**   *n.* **cards**
> *n.* **baseball**   *n.* **chess**
> *n.* **tennis**
> *n.* **basketball**

Q. Do you like sport ?
Q. What is your favourite sport ?

Q. Can you play tennis ?
Q. Can you play it well ?

Q. Is chess an easy game to play ?

Q. Do you ever play cards ?
Q. Do you ever play for money ?

Q. What kind of animals like playing games with people ?

> *v.* **to make**
> We **make** a cup of tea with hot water, tea and milk.
> They **make** a lot of computers in America.

Q. What do you use to make a cup of tea ?   *we use tea to*

Q. What do you use to make a **cheese** sandwich ?

Q. Which countries make a lot of :
 a. films ?   b. computers ?   c. cameras ?

Q. Do they make cars in your country ?
Q. What kind of cars do they make ?

Q. Can you make a cup of tea with cold water ?

Q. Who usually makes dinner in your house ?

gerund (2)   *n.* **preposition**

Before, after, in, on, with, without, of, from and for are **prepositions**.

When there is a verb after a **preposition** we use the gerund.
eg.   I eat breakfast **before** go**ing** to work.
       You can't speak English well **without** study**ing**.

Q.   Can you speak English well without studying ? *No. I Can't*

Q.   Can you eat rice before cooking it ? *NO*

Q.   Do you ever drink beer before coming to school ?

Q.   Can you sleep after drinking a cup of coffee ?

Q.   Is it easy to live in a country without knowing the language well ?
       NO. It ist

prep. **up**   *prep.* **down**
 v. **to stand up**   *v.* **to sit down**

Q.   Are you standing up or sitting down ?

Q.   Do you stand up when you eat ?

Q.   Do I sit down when I teach ?

Q.   Do you sit down when you have a shower ? *NO. I don't sit down when I hav~*

Q.   Put your hand up.
Q.   Can you put it down now.

Q.   What is that up there ? - (teacher points)
Q.   What is that down there ?- (teacher points)

n. **stairs**   **upstairs**   **downstairs**

Q.   Are there stairs in this school ? *yes. There are stirs in this school*

Q.   Do flats usually have stairs ?   *No. flats don't.*

Q.   In a house, which rooms are usually upstairs and which rooms are usually downstairs ?

Q.   In a house, is the kitchen usually upstairs or downstairs ? *In a house they down stairs*
       in a honse   *Her*

n. **top**   *n.* **bottom**
at the top of   **at the bottom of**
There is a restaurant **at the top of** the Eiffel Tower.
I usually write my name **at the bottom** of a letter.

Q.   Is there a classroom at the bottom of the stairs in this school ?
       No There is't
Q.   When you write a letter, where do you write your address ?

Q.   When you write a letter, where do you write your name ? *when I write a letter.*
       when I write   *I write my name at the Bottom*
       I   I. write at the Bottom
               my name.

the moment ~ 하자마자
as soon as.

split - level.

at the moment = now

Q.   What are you doing at the moment ?

Q.   Where are you living at the moment ?

Q.   Are you using a computer at the moment ? *No. I'm not.*

> *v.* **to be** + adjective   *adj.* **happy**
>   *adj.* **sad / unhappy**
> We can use adjectives after the verb to be.
> eg.   I **am happy** today.
>   A cold drink **is nice** on a hot day.

Q.   Are you happy at the moment ?
Q.   Quite happy or very happy ?

Q.   Do you think hot coffee is nice on a cold day ?

Q.   Are you unhappy when you can't speak to your friends ? *Yes*

Q.   Can you give me an example of a sad film ?

Q.   Is it hot or cold today ?   *warm.*

Q.   Is this a nice colour ?

> *adj.* **hungry**   *adj.* **thirsty**

Q.   Are you hungry/thirsty at the moment ?

Q.   Are you hungry before eating dinner ? *yes.*

Q.   Are you hungry after eating a big dinner ? *no*

Q.   What do you like drinking when you are very thirsty ?

Q.   What do you like eating when you are very hungry ?

> *n.* **infinitive**
> To go, to dance, to speak, and to ask are **infinitive verbs**.

부정사

Q.   Give me an example of an infinitive ?*   *To   speak*

Q.   Give me an example of :
      a. an infinitive.   *I   speak English*
      b. the present simple.
      c. the present continuous.   *I am speaking English.*
      d. a gerund.
                                                       I like speaking   "

v. **to want + infinitive**

We can use a noun or the infinitive after the verb 'to want'.

eg. When I am hungry I **want** *to eat.*
    When I am thirsty I **want** *to drink.*

Q. Do you have a lot of money ?

Q. Do you want a lot of money ?

Q. Do you want to speak English well ?

Q. What job do you want to do ? *I want to be ~ .*

Q. What do you want to do after the lesson ?

Q. How long do you want to study English ?

Q. Why do you want to study English ?

Q. Do you want to do the same job as your mother/father ? *No. I don't.*

v. **to walk**

prep. **to**	*prep.* **by**	
n. **train**	*n.* **bus**	*n.* **plane**
n. **underground**	*n.* **bike / bicycle**	*n.* **ship**

eg. We go **to** America **by** plane.
    I go **to** work **by** train.
    He **walks** to school.
    She goes home **by** bus.

Q. Do you walk to school ?
Q. How do you come to school ?
A. I come to school by ...

Q. How do you go home ?
A. I go home by ...

Q. Do you like walking ?

Q. Do you walk quickly when you come to school ?

Q. How do people usually go to work in your city ?

Q. Do people usually go to America by ship ? *No. people don't usuall.*

Q. Is there an underground in your city ?
Q. Do you ever use it ?

Q. **What do you use to wash your face ?**

Q. **Can you speak English without thinking in your language ?**

Q. **Stand up please.**
Q. **Do you want to sit down now ?**

Q. **Do you want to answer an easy question or a difficult question ?**

n. **foot** (*pl.* feet)   n. **finger**   n. **thumb**   n. **toe**

Q.   What is the plural of foot ?

Q.   How many feet do you have ?

Q.   How many fingers and thumbs do you have ?

Q.   Do you ever eat with with your fingers ?
Q.   What kind of food ?

Q.   Do you always wash between your toes ?

v. **to wear**   n. **hat**   n. **scarf**   n. **cardigan**
                        n. **gloves**   n. **coat**   n. **boots**

Q.   What clothes are you wearing ?

Q.   What clothes do you wear when it is very cold ?

Q.   What kind of people wear gloves for work ?

Q.   Do you ever wear a hat ?
Q.   Is he/she wearing a hat ?

Q.   Do you prefer wearing shoes or boots ?

Q.   What clothes do you wear at work ?

Q.   Do you wear the same kind of clothes as :
       a. your mother/father   b. (famous person)*

n. **jeans**   n. **dress**   n. **skirt**   n. **shorts**

Q.   Are you wearing shorts ?
Q.   When do people wear shorts ?

Q.   Are you wearing a dress ?

Q.   Do you like wearing jeans ?

Q.   Do you prefer jeans or trousers ?
Q.   Which are you wearing ?

Q.   Do you prefer wearing trousers or a skirt ?

n. **pair of** + **noun** = 2 of the same thing
We say **a pair of** socks / shoes / boots / gloves / trousers

Q.   How many pairs of shoes do you have ?   I have of pairs of shoes

Q.   Do you have a pair of gloves ?
Q.   What colour are they ?

Q.   Are you wearing two pairs of socks ?

Q.   How many pairs of jeans do you have ?

n. **glasses**   *n.* **sunglasses**
a pair of glasses/sunglasses

Q. Do you wear glasses ?
Q. How many pairs of glasses do you have ?

Q. Do you wear glasses to :
a. watch television ?   b. read ?

Q. Do you have a pair of sunglasses ?

v. **to mean**   *n.* **meaning**
The word 'pair' **means** two of the same thing.
A **tick** (√) **means** the answer is right.
A **cross** (X) **means** the answer is wrong.

Q. Does a tick (√) mean right or wrong ?

Q. What does a cross (X) mean ?

Q. Do you know the meaning of these words ?
a. pair   b. the washing up   c. parents   d. **weekend***   e. **penguin***

Q. What do these letters mean :
a. UK ?   b. USA ?   c. UN?

NB.   When you don't understand a word you can ask :
What does ... mean ?
eg.   Q.   What does pair mean ?
        A.   Pair means two of the same thing.

Q. Ask me what these words mean :
a.**huge**   b. **tiny**   c. **dislike***

---

some and **any**
We use a/an with singular, countable nouns. (**a** book, **an** animal)
We use **any/some** with plural and uncountable nouns.
We use **any** in questions.
plural noun -   Q.   Do you have **any** English friends ?
uncountable noun -   Q.   Do you have **any** bread ?

We use **some** in positive sentences.
plural noun -   A.   Yes, I have **some** English friends.
uncountable noun   A.   Yes, I have **some** bread.

We use **not any** in negative sentences.
                                        I do**n't** have **any** money.
                                        There are**n't any** socks in the drawer.

a. an — singular + cantable noms
any/some — plural + uncantable nome
any — in questions (?)

exercise

*Write **a**, **an**, **any** or **some** in these sentences.*

some. (+) positive sentences
not any (−) Negative. sentences.

1. Do you have *any* brothers or sisters ?

2. Are there *any* big cities in your country ?

3. Do you know *any* English people ?

4. Is there *any* milk in the fridge ?

5. Is there *a* restaurant in your street ?

6. There is *an* apple in the fruit bowl.

7. There are *some* plates in the sink.

8. There is *some* money on the table.

9. There isn't *any* butter in the fridge.

10. Do you have *any* beer ?

11. He doesn't have *any* friends.

12. She has *some* stamps in her drawer.

Q. Are there any restaurants in your street ?

Q. Do you have any food in your fridge ?

Q. Do you know any English newspapers ?

Q. Do you have any wine at home ?

Q. Do you have any classical music at home ?

Q. Do you know any English people ?
Q. Are there any English people in this room ?

Q. Do you have any food in your bag ?

Are you => have it

adj. **new**

!! We use **new** for things and **young** for people and animals.
The opposite of **new** is **old**.

Q. Are your shoes old or new ?
Q. Quite old/new or very old/new ?

Q. Do you ever wear old jeans ?

Q. Do you have any new clothes at home ?

Q. Do you like old, black and white films ?

Q. Are there any new students in the class today ?

n. **shop**   n. **shopping**   v. **to go shopping**

Q. Do you like shopping ?

Q. What is your favourite kind of shop ?

Q. Are there any shops in this street ?
Q. What kind of shops ?   *There are.*

Q. Do you go shopping a lot ?   *yes. I go shopping alot*

Q. When you go shopping for clothes do you like going with a friend ?

I don't like going with friend ?

v. **to buy**	v. **to sell**
n. **supermarket**	n. **department store**
n. **newsagent**	n. **market**

Q.   Where do you buy your food ?   *I buy my food form supermarket.*

Q.   Do you often buy new clothes ?   *some times*

Q.   What kind of shops sell newspapers and cigarettes ?

Q.   Are there any department stores in this city ?
Q.   Give me an example.

Q.   Is there a market in this city ?

Q.   What kind of things do they sell in :
a. a shoe shop ?   b. a market ?   c. a department store ?

Q.   Where can you buy :
a. books ?   b. stamps ?   c. **soap*** ?

How much ... ?

Q.   About how much is a newspaper in your country ?

Q.   About how much is a bottle of good wine ?

Q.   How much is a cup of coffee in a cafe ?

Q.   How much is a CD in your country ?

adj. **expensive**	adj. **cheap**
n. **Champagne**	

Q.   Is Champagne cheap ?
Q.   How much is a bottle of very good Champagne ?

Q.   Give me an example of :
a. a cheap car.   b. an expensive car.

Q.   Do you often eat in expensive restaurants ?

Q.   Do you think this school is expensive ?

Q.   Where can you buy cheap food and clothes ?

v. **to open**	v. **to close**

I am **closing** my book.
I am **opening** my book.

Q.   What am I doing ?

Q.   What am I doing ?

Q. Open/Close your book please.

Q. What is he/she doing ?

Q. Do the shops open on Sundays in this city ?
    yes .

Q. What time do the shops close in your country ?

          adj. **open**   *adj.* **closed**

Q. Is my book open ?

Q. Is my book closed ?

Q. Is this school closed on Sundays ?

Q. Where can you buy food when the supermarkets are closed ?

---

pronouns

We use **pronouns** when we don't use a noun.
We can say :   **John** is from Scotland.
or we can say :   **He** is from Scotland

He is a subject **pronoun**.
The **subject pronouns** are :   I, you, he, she, it, we, you, they.

---

exercise

Write the answers to the questions using subject pronnouns.

eg.   Q.   Is London a big city ?
       A.   Yes, **it** is a big city.

1.   Is Paris in France ?

      Yes. it is a France

2.   Does your father have a job ?   *yes   He has a job?*

3.   Does your mother have a car ?   *yes. She has a car*

4.   Do dogs eat meat ?   *yes They eat meat*
      yes dogs eat meat ?

5.   Do Italian people eat a lot of rice ?   *Yes.*

      No. They don't   people eat a lot of rice

Q. Do you have a dog ?
Q. Does it eat meat ?

Q. What city are you from ?
Q. Is it clean or dirty ?

Q. Do you have a brother ?
Q. Does he have a car ?

Q. Do you have a sister ?
Q. Is she nice ?

Q. Do Americans speak English ?

Q. Can your mother cook very well ?
Q. And your father ?

Unit 6

n. **weekend** = Saturday and Sunday   *n.* **nightclub**

Q. What does the noun weekend mean ?

Q. What do you like doing at the weekend ?

Q. Do you ever go to nightclubs at the weekend ?

Q. What do people do at nightclubs ? *They deuce*

Q. Do you ever work at the weekend ?

Q. What is your favourite day of the week ?

Q. Is this school open at the weekend ? *No. this is*

n. **skin**   *adj.* **hard**   *adj.* **soft**

Q. Is your head soft ?
Q. Is your face soft ?

Q. Is your skin soft after a hot bath ?

Q. What kind of food is hard before cooking and soft after cooking ?

Q. Do you prefer sleeping on a hard bed or a soft bed ?

Q. What kind of clothes do we make from animal skin ?

v. **to add** (to)
Some people **add** lemon to tea.
We **add** the letter 's' to a noun to make a regular plural.   eg. cat / cats.

Q. What do we add to a noun to make a regular plural ?
Q. Give me an example.   *We add*

Q. What do people often add to tea and coffee ?

Q. What letters do we add to make these words plural ?
    a. pen   b. child   c. potato *s*

Q. What letters do we add to spell these words ?*
    a. difficul...   b. colou..   c. orang..

aelou – Vowels

v. **to begin**   *v.* **to end**
n. **the beginning**   *n.* **the end**
The alphabet **begins** with the letter A and **ends** with letter Z.

Q. What letter do regular plural nouns end with ?

Revision

Q. What letters does your name begin and end with ?

Q. What do I say at the beginning of the lesson ? *you say*
Q. What do I say at the end of the lesson ? *you say*

Q. Are you always in the classroom when the lesson begins ?

Q. What do you generally do when the lesson ends ?
I generall. go

---

possessive adjectives

adj. **possessive**

NB.   We use a **possessive adjective** before a noun.

my	This is **my** shirt.
your	That is **your** book
his/her	That is **his/her** pen
its	
our	This is **our** classroom
your	I am **your** teacher
their	I am **their** teacher

Q. Is this my arm ?
Q. Is this my leg ?

Q. What colour are your eyes ?

Q. Who are your teachers ?

Q. What colour are his/her shoes ?

Q. What is his/her name ?

Q. Is this our classroom ?

Q. Am I their teacher ?

Q. What are their nationalities ?

v. **to belong** (to)
This is my book, it **belongs** to me.
Those chairs **belong** to this school.

Q. Does that chair belong to you ?

Q. Does your house belong to you ?

Q. What things in the classroom belong to you ?

possessive (2)

possessive 's   Whose ...?
The book belongs to Richard, so we say it is Richard's book.
Richard's book is blue.

We use **whose** to make a question.
Q.   **Whose** book is this ?
A.   It is Richard's book.
Q.   **Whose** bag is that ?
A.   That is Clare's bag.

Use the student's name in your answers.*

Q.   Whose book is that ?
A.   It is ...'s book ?

Q.   Whose shoes are those ?
A.   They are ...'s shoes ?

Q.   Whose eyes are brown ?
A.   ...'s eyes are brown.

Q.   Whose hair is black ?

Q.   What colour are ....'s trousers ?

Q.   Is ....'s hair long or short ?

Slice of bread

Loaf

loaves

       adj. **married**   *adj.* **single**   **Mr**   **Mrs**   **Miss**   **Ms**

Q.   Are you married or single ?

Q.   Are any of your brothers or sisters married ?

Q.   Why do some women use Ms ?

       n. **husband**   *n.* **wife***

Q.   Can a woman have two husbands in your country ?

Q.   Are any of your brothers or sisters married ?
Q.   What is his wife's name ? / What is her husband's name ?

       n. **grandparents**   *n.* **grandmother**   *n.* **grandfather**

Q.   What do the words 'grandmother' and 'grandfather' mean ?

Q.   What are your grandparents' names ?
Q.   Where do they live ?

n. **son**　　　*n.* **daughter**

Q. Are you a son or daughter ?

Q. When you have a child, do you want a son or a daughter ?

adj. **beautiful**　　*adj.* **ugly**

Q. Can you think of a beautiful building in this city ?

Q. Can you think of an ugly building in this city ?

Q. Is it a beautiful day today ?

Q. Which animals do you think are ugly ?

n. **syllable**

[ˈsɪləbl]

Some words have 1 **syllable** : man, boy, good, young.
Some words have 2 **syllables** : wo-man, bad-ly, hap-py.
Some words have 3 **syllables** : beau-ti-ful, al-pha-bet, sin-gu-lar.

Q. How many syllables does the word 'man' have ?

Q. How many syllables does the word 'happy' have?

Q. How many syllables does the word 'beautiful' have?

Q. How many syllables does your name have ?

n. **comparatives**

prep. **than**
We make **comparatives** by adding the letters '**er**' to adjectives with 1 syllable.
We always use the word '**than**' after a **comparative**.

adjective	comparative
old	**old*er* than**
young	**young*er* than**
big	**bigg*er** than**
small	**small*er* than**

eg.　My mother isn't young, but she is **young*er* than** my father.
　　Paris isn't a small city, but it is **small*er* than** London.

Q. Is your mother older or younger than your father ?

Q. Is your city bigger or smaller than London ?

Q. Do you think you are older or younger than me ?

Q. Which countries are bigger than your country ?

adjective	comparative
hot	hot**ter* than**
cold	cold**er than**

Q. Is England hotter or colder than your country ?

Q. Which countries are colder than your country ?

Q. Is it usually hotter in the mornings or the afternoons ?

We can make comparatives by adding the letters **er** to adjectives of 2 syllables when they end in the letter **y** :

adjective	comparative
happy	happ**ier than**
dirty	dirt**ier than**
easy	eas**ier than**

NB.   We use the letters **ier** and <u>not</u> **yer** for these comparatives.

Q. Do you think shopping is easier than studying ?

Q. Are your shoes cleaner or dirtier than my shoes ?

Q. Are you happier at the end or the beginning of the week ?

adjective	comparative
tall	tall**er than**
short	short**er than**
light	light**er than**
heavy	heav**ier than**

Q. Are basketball players usually tall or short ?

Q. Are you taller or shorter than me/him/her ?

Q. Do you think your chair is lighter than the table ?

Q. Give me an example of a very heavy animal ?

Q. Are there any animals that are heavier than elephants ?

musical instruments   *n.* **guitar**   *n.* **drums**

n. **piano**   *n.* **violin**

Q. Give me an example of a musical instrument.

Q. Can you play any musical instruments ?
Q. Which instruments can you play ?

Q. What kind of instruments do people play in :
   a. classical music ?   b. pop music ?

thing pronouns

pron. **anything**   _pron._ **something**

We use a pronoun when we don't use a noun.
When we ask a question with any, we use any + a noun.
We can ask :

  Q.   Do you have **any books** in your bag ?
        But when you don't use a noun we use the pronoun **anything**.

eg.   Q.   Do you have **anything** in bag ?

We use **anything** in questions.
We use **something** in positive sentences
We use **not anything** in negative sentences.

eg .   Q.   Do you have **anything** in my pocket ?
      +A.   Yes, I have **something** in my pocket.
      -A.   No, I do not have **anything** in my pocket.

NB.   These pronouns are **singular**.*
eg.   Q.   Do you have anything in your bag ?
      A.   Yes, I have a book in my bag.

Answer these questions using a noun, not a pronoun.

_Q._   Do you have anything in your pocket ? _yes. I have something in my pocket_ _(coin and c)_

_Q._   Is there anything heavy in the classroom ? _there is (   ) in the classroom_

_Q._   Are you wearing anything expensive ? _yes. I am wearing something expensive._

_Q._   Give me an example of something :
      a. beautiful. _flower_   b. ugly.

_Q._   Do you have anything to read in your bag ? _Yes. I have something to read in my bag_

_Q._   Do you have anything nice to eat at home ? _Yes_   _No, I haven't_   _. nice to eat at home_

_Q._   Is there anything you don't like eating ? _yes. There is_   _yes, I don't like eating_

_Q._   Is there anything you want to ask me ? _yes. I have, I_

_Q._   Give me an example of :
      a. something you want to buy.
      b. something you keep in a drawer.
      c. something you like doing at the weekend.
      d. something you drink with dinner.
      e. something you eat for breakfast.
      f. something you don't like doing.

people pronouns

pron. **someone** *pron.* **anyone** *pron.* **not anyone**

We use **anything** and **something** for things.
We use **anyone** and **someone** for people.

eg. Q. Is there **anyone** in the bathroom ?
+A. Yes there is **someone** in the bathroom.
-A. No, there is**n't anyone** in the bathroom.

eg. Q. Do you know **anyone** who lives in Paris ?
A. Yes, my brother lives in Paris.

Answer these questions using a noun, not a pronoun.

Q. Do you know anyone in London ?

Q. Do you know anyone who lives in America ?

Q. Is there anyone eating in this classroom ?

Q. Is there anyone in the classroom who can speak English very well ?

Q. Can anyone here play a musical instrument ?

Q. Does anyone here have a dog ?

Q. Does anyone want to ask me a question ?

v. **to see** *v.* **to hear**
We **see** with our eyes.
We **hear** with our ears.

Q. Can you see anything red in the classroom ?

Q. Can you hear me speaking ?

Q. What is the first thing you hear in the morning ?

Q. What is the first thing you see when you open your eyes in the morning ?

listen and hear

We **hear** things generally but when we <u>want</u> to hear something we **listen to** it.
eg. When I **listen**, I can **hear** the cars in the street and people talking.

Q. Can you hear the cars in the street ?
Q. Are you listening to the cars ?

Q. When you want to know what someone is saying, do you listen or hear ?

Q. Listen, what can you hear ?

n. **shape**   n. **cirle**   n. **square**
adj. **round**   adj. **square**

Q. What shape is this ?*

Q. Can you see anything square in this room ?

Q. Can you see anything round in this room ?

Q. What shape is :
 a. a ball ?   b. a plate ?   c. a teabag ?

n. **triangle**   adj. **triangular**   n. **rectangle**   adj. **rectangular**

Q. What shape is this ?*

Q. What shape is this room ?

Q. Can you see anything rectangular in this room ?

Q. Can you see anything triangular in this room ?
Q. Can you think of anything triangular ?

---

questions with **have got**

We can use **do** to make a question with the verb **to have** :
eg.   Q.   **Do** you **have** a pen ?

But sometimes we use the word **got** to make a question with the verb to have :

have + subject pronoun + got
eg.   Q.   **Have** you   **got**   a   pen ?
We usually use **got** in the answer:
        + A. Yes, I have **got** a pen.
        - A. No, I have not **got** a pen.

Q. Have you got a pen ?
A. Yes, I have got a pen.

Q. Have you got any books on your table ?
A. Yes I have got some books on my table.

---

n. **contraction**
I have got = I**'ve** got
I have not got = I have**n't** got
he has got = he**'s** got
he has not got = he has**n't** got

We usually use **contractions** with **have got**.

Q. What is the contraction of :   a. I have got ?   b. he has not got ?
                                   c. they have got ?   d. we have not got ?

Q. What is the contraction of :   a. I am ?   b. he is not ?
                                   c. they cannot ?   d. he does not ?

Use contractions in your answers to these questions.

Q. Have you got a cat ? *No. I haven't got a cat*

Q. Have you got a dog ?

Q. Have you got anything in your pocket ?
A. Yes, I've got something in my pocket.
Q. What have you got ? *I have got ~*

Q. Is he/she from Scotland ? *he/she isn't from scotland.*

Q. Are they from America ? *No. they aren't from America?*

Q. Have you got anything expensive in your bag ? *I have got someting expensive in my bag*

Q. What has he/she got in her pocket ? - Ask. *your.*

to be good *at* something

Q. What sports are you good at ? *I good at ballyball Golf.*

Q. Are you good at cooking ?

Q. Are you good at writing with your left hand ?

Q. Are you good at spelling English words ?

v. **to run**	adjective	adverb
	fast	**fast** (irregular)
	slow	**slowly**

Q. In which sports do people run ? *people run.*

Q. What kind of animals can run very fast ?

Q. Is walking faster or slower than running ?

Q. Is a bus faster than a train ?

Q. Give me an example of a fast car.

adj. **warm**   *adj.* **cool**
Spring is **warm**, summer is hot.
Autumn is **cool**, winter is cold.

Q. Is it hot, warm, cool or cold today ?

Q. In summer, is it cooler in the morning or the afternoon ?

Q. Is it warmer in spring than in summer ?

Q. Do you wear warm clothes in winter ? *yes I wear warm clothes in winter*
Q. Give me some examples of warm clothes.

Q. On a very hot day, do you prefer a hot bath or a cool shower ?

n. **holiday**   **to go on holiday**
adv. **abroad**

Q. Do you like going on holiday ?

Q. Do you prefer going on holiday abroad or in your country ?

Q. Do you ever go on holiday in winter ?

Q. Do you like playing sports on holiday ?

Q. What do you play ?

Q. What kind of holidays are :
a. expensive ?   b. cheap ?

Q. In what month do people usually go on holiday in your country ?

July to August.

adj. **foreign**   *n.* **foreigner**

Q. Are you a foreigner in this country ?

Q. What foreign languages can you speak ?

Q. Do you like going to foreign countries ? *Yes I like it.*

Q. What kinds of foreign food do people eat in your country ?

n. **passport**   *n.* **visa**

Q. What colour is your passport ?

Q. Have you got your passport with you *me* ?

Q. Do you have any visas in your passport ?

Q. For which countries ?

n. **beach**   *n.* **mountains**

Q. Which do you prefer, a holiday on the beach or in the mountains ?

Q. Are there any beaches near your city ? *my city is*
No. There aren't any beaches near my city

Q. Are there any mountains near your city ?

Q. In what season do people often go on holiday :
a. to the beach ?   b. to the mountains ?

Q. What kind of clothes do people wear :
a. on the beach ?   b. in the mountains ?

Q. What kind of sports do people play on the beach ?

v. **to ski**

Q. Can you ski ?

Q. Can you ski well ?

Q. In what season do people go skiing ? *winter*

Q. What is the meaning of :
  a. a pair of skis ?   b. a pair of ski-boots ?   c. water skiing ?

v. **to swim**   n. **sea**   n. **river**

Q. Can you swim ?

Q. Can you swim well ?

Q. Is there a river in this city ?

Q. What is its name ?

Q. Do people swim in it ? *No. They don't swim*

Q. Do you prefer swimming in the sea or a swimming pool ?

Q. Which is faster, skiing or swimming ?

v. **to enjoy** + gerund

Q. Do you enjoy going on holiday ?

Q. What sports do you enjoy playing ?

Q. Do you enjoy swimming when the water is warm ? *yes I enjoy*

Q. What kind of music do you enjoy listening to ?

Q. What do you enjoy doing at the weekend ? *I*

adj. **hard** = difficult

Q. Do you think this book is hard ?

Q. Do you think learning a foreign language is hard ? *yes I think so*

Q. Do you think writing English is harder than speaking English ?

adv. **hard** = a lot
Hard is an adjective and an irregular adverb.

Q. Do your parents work hard ? *my parents work hard*

Q. Do you always study hard at home ?

Q. Do people usually enjoy working hard ? *yes they usually*
  I think people usually

n. **weather**   *v.* **to rain**   *n.* **rain**

v. **to snow**   *n.* **snow**

NB.   We always use the pronoun **it** for weather.

eg.   **It** is a sunny day.

It is snowing.

Q.   Is it raining ?

Q.   Does it ever rain a lot in your country ? yes it does rains ~

Q.   In which season ?   Summer

Q.   Do you enjoy walking in the rain ?

Q.   Does it snow in the mountains in winter ? Yes it snow ~

Q.   What sports can we play when it snows ?

Q.   What kind of games do children enjoy playing in the snow ?

n. **sky**   *n.* **sun**   *adj.* **sunny**

n. **cloud**   *adj.* **cloudy**

adj. **rainy***

Q.   Can you see the sky from where you are stting ?

Q.   What colour is the sky today ?

Q.   Is it cloudy today ?

Q.   What do you like doing on a:

a. sunny day ?   b. rainy day ?

Q.   Does your country have a rainy season ? Yes. It have has.

n. **wind**   *adj.* **windy**

Q.   Is it windy today ?

Q.   Is it difficult to use an umbrella on a windy day ?   Yes

Q.   Do you like going to the beach on a very windy day ? No

Unit 7

the present: today

Today is the **present**.

the past: yesterday

Yesterday is the **past**.

Q. Is today the present or the past ?

Q. Is yesterday the present or the past ?

the past simple tense

We use the **past simple** for an action in the past.

We make the past simple tense by adding the letters **ed** to the end of a regular verb.

eg. I play**ed** tennis yesterday.

He watch**ed** television yesterday.

present	past	present	past
walk	walk**ed**	live	liv**ed**
ask	ask**ed**	prefer	prefer**red**
use	us**ed**	want	want**ed**
like	lik**ed**	work	work**ed**
listen	listen**ed**	cook	cook**ed**
watch	watch**ed**	count	count**ed**

did

The past simple of do is **did**.

We use **did** to make a question in the past simple.

Q. **Did** you watch television yesterday ?
A. Yes, I watch**ed** television yesterday.

Q. **Did** he watch television yesterday?
A. Yes, he watch**ed** television yesterday.

NB. Did you watch ? NOT ~~Did you watched ?~~

Answer these questions using the past simple tense.

Q. Did you watch television yesterday ?
A. Yes, I watched television yesterday.

Q. Did you study English yesterday ?
A. Yes, I studied yesterday.

Q. Did I ask you any questions yesterday ?

Q. Did you wash your face yesterday ?

Q. Did I use the board yesterday ?

Q. Did you play sport at school ?

---

negative answers in the past

To make a negative answer in the past we use **did not** ... .

eg. Q. **Did** you watch television last night ?

   A. No, I **did not** watch television last night.

NB. The contraction of did not is **didn't**.

Q. Did you play cricket at school ?

Q. Did you work last Sunday ?

Q. Did you use a computer yesterday ?

Q. Did you study Spanish last week ?

Q. Make a question using the past simple.

exercise

Write the past tense of these verbs.

1. I .*walked*....... (walk) to school yesterday.

2. My sister .*uced*............. (use) my computer on Tuesday.

3. They .*didn't like*. (not like) the film.

4. We ....*danced*...... (dance) to slow music in a night club.

5. We ..*did not lived*. (not live) in London in 1997.

6. I .*did worked*... (work) in a restaurant in June.

7. I ...*not didn't l*. (not <u>listen</u>) to the radio yesterday.

8. She ....*cooked*..... (cook) Italian food for dinner.

---

present : this week   this month   this year
past :   last week   last month   last year

last week = the week before this week.

Q. Did you use a pen last week ?

Q. Did you enjoy your last holiday ?

Q. Did you play any games last week ?

Q. Did you work last Sunday ?

Q. Did you watch television last night ?

irregular verbs

Some verbs are **regular** in the past and some are **irregular**.

present	past simple
have	**had**
go	**went**
come	**came**
wear	**wore**
speak	**spoke**

Q.   What is the past simple of to do ?   *did*

Q.   What is the past simple of to have ?
Q.   Did you have a lesson last week ?   *No I haven't. didn't*

Q.   What is the past simple of to go ?   *went*
Q.   Did you go home after the lesson yesterday ?

Q.   What is the past simple of to come ?
Q.   How did you come to school yesterday ?
A.   I came to·school by train, bus...etc.

Q.   What is the past simple of to wear ?
Q.   What did you wear yesterday ?

Q.   Did you speak English last year ?

Q.   Did he/she speak English last year ? - Ask.

exercise

Write the past simple of these verbs.

1.   I ....*had*.......... (to have) dinner with my friends last night.

2.   They .... (to go) to the cinema last week.

3.   She .... (to come) to my house yesterday.

4.   I .... (to speak) French at school.

5.   He .... (to wear) jeans when he .... (to go) to the cinema.

adv. **ago**
ten minutes **ago** = ten minutes in the past
five weeks **ago** = five weeks in the past
three years **ago** = three years in the past
eg.   I spoke to my friend ten minutes **ago**.
      He came to England five weeks **ago**.
      They went to Paris three years **ago**.

Q.   Did you speak English 5 years ago ?

Q.   When did you first come to this school ?

Q. When did you last cook dinner ?

Q. When did you last do the washing up ?

Q. Did you study English at school ?
Q. How long ago ?

The verb **to be** is irregular in the simple past.

I **was**
you **were**
he/she **was**
it **was**
we **were**
you **were**
they **were**

Q. What is the past of the verb to be ?
A. The past of the verb to be is I was, you were, he was, she was, ... etc.

Q. Were you here yesterday ?

Q. Was he/she here yesterday ?

Q. Was I your teacher three weeks ago ?

Q. Were you in this city two months ago ?

Q. Was there a film on television last night ?
Q. Did you watch it ?
Q. Was it good ?

Q. Were you here last Sunday ?

Q. How many students were here yesterday ?

n. **time**   **first time**
                       last time
eg.   The **first time** I **had** Chinese food **was** three years ago.
      The **last time** I **cooked** dinner **was** on Saturday night.

Q. When was the first time you studied English ?

Q. When was the first time you used a computer ?   was

Q. When was the last time you spoke to your parents ?

Q. When was the last time you spoke your language ?   was

n. **subject**

ps

hardly

n. **science**   *n.* **maths** (mathematics)   *n.* **geography** *2/2/.*

n. **history**   *n.* **English**

Q. Did you study English at school ?

Q. What subjects did you study at school ?

Q. What was your favourite subject at school ?

Q. Did you study maths at school ?
Q. Did you like it ?

Q. In what subject do we study the past ?

Here are some irregular verbs.
think   **thought**
understand   **understood**
teach   **taught**
read   **read**

Q. What is the past of teach ?
Q. Did I teach you last week ?

Q. What is the past of understand ?
Q. Did you understand your first lesson at this school ?

Q. What is the past of read ?
Q. When was the last time you read a newspaper ?

Q. What is the past of think ?

adj. **interesting**   *adj.* **boring**

Q. What subjects did you think were interesting at school ? *I. thock mas was.*

Q. What subjects did you think were boring at school ?

Q. Give me an example of an interesting :
    a. film.   b. book.   c. person.

Q. Do you think watching sport on television is interesting or boring ?

v. **to remember**   *v.* **to forget**

Q. Can you remember my name ?

Q. What is the opposite of to remember ?

Q. Can you remember the telephone number of this school ?

Q. Do you ever forget to call your parents ?

Q. Do old people often forget things ?

Q. Can you always remember which is left and which is right ?

Some more irregular verbs :
know	**knew**
write	**wrote**
forget	**forgot**
spell	**spelt**

Q. What is the past of to know ?
Q. Did you know me two weeks ago ?

Q. What is the past of to write ?
Q. Did you write any letters last week ? I was
Q. Who did you write to ?

Q. What is the past of to forget ?
Q. Do you ever forget your English books ?
Q. When was the last time you forgot your English books ?

Q. What is the past of to spell ?
Q. Spell my name.

Q. Did he/she spell my name right ?

exercise
Write the past tense of these verbs.

1. I .... (to know) the answer to the question.

2. He .... (to read) the newspaper and .... (to go) to bed.

3. She .... (to write) a letter to her parents yesterday.

4. They .... (to be) happy when they .... (to be) children.

5. I .... (to watch) the news in English and I .... (to understand) it.

6. He .... (to forget) his mother's address.

7. Yesterday he .... (to spell) my name wrong.

8. He .... (to think) the film .... (to be) very good.

Some more irregular verbs
make	**made**
sing	**sang**
drink	**drank**
buy	**bought**

Q. Do you ever make dinner at home ?
Q. When was the last time you made dinner ?

Q. Who sang :
    a. Imagine b. Help!

difference

Q. When was the last time you went to the pub ?

Q. What did you drink ?

Q. Did you go shopping last weekend ?

Q. What did you buy ?

---

years, **dates** and **numbers**

number		adjective	
1	one	first	= 1st.
2	two	second	= 2nd.
3	three	third	= 3rd.
4	four	fourth	= 4th.
5	five	fifth	= 5th.
6	six	sixth	= 6th.
7	seven	seventh	= 7th.
8	eight	eighth	= 8th.
9	nine	ninth	= 9th.
10	ten	tenth	= 10th.

A very easy way to remember how to say and write these adjective numbers is that they end in '**th**'.
BUT we say: **1st, 2nd and 3rd**. or **21st, 22nd, 23rd** or **31st, 32nd, and 33rd etc**.

Q. What is the first day of the week ? It is Sunday

Q. What is the third day of the week ?

Q. What is the fifth day of the week ?

Q. What is the last day of the week ?   The _ of

Q. What is the first month of the year ?

Q. What is the eighth month of the year ?

Q. What is the tenth month of the year ?

Q. What is the last month of the year ?

---

n. **the year**
When we say the year in English we make two numbers :
1965 = 19 - 65 (nineteen - sixty-five)
1939 = 19 - 39 (nineteen - thirty-nine)
2010 = 20 - 10 (twenty - ten)

Q. Say these years: 1965   1922   1969   2011   1971   1939*

Q. What year is it ?

Q. What year was it last year ?

It was 1998

Q. What year was it 10 years ago ? *It was 1990*

Q. What year did your parents get married ? *They got married in 1960*

> *n.* **the date**
>
> *we write* : 4th August   *we say* : **the** fourth **of** August
>
> *we write* : 19th May   *we say* : **the** nineteenth **of** May
>
> *we write* : 10th October   *we say* : **the** tenth **of** October

Q. Say these dates :
  a. 25th December   b. 1st January
  c. 19th November   d. 14th February

Q. What is today's date ?   *18th April*

Q. What was yesterday's date ? *19.*

Q. What was the date two days ago ?

> *n.* **birthday**   *n.* **Christmas**

Q. When is Christmas ?
A. Christmas is on the 25th of December.

Q. When is your birthday ?
A. My birthday is on ...

Q. When is his/her birthday ? - Ask.

Q. Can you remember your seventh birthday ?

> *v.* **to be born**   *past simple* = I **was** born, you **were** born *etc.*
>
> eg.   My mother **was** born <u>on</u> 12th July,1937.
>   I **was** born <u>on</u> 20th January, 1977.

Q. When were you born ? *I was born*

Q. Where were you born ?

Q. When was he/she born ? - Ask.

Q. Who was born on Christmas Day about 2000 years ago ?

> *n.* **life**   *n.* **death**

Q. Is your life interesting or boring ?

Q. Give me an example of someone who had a very interesting life.

Q. Do you think there is life after death ?

    Yes. I think so
    No. I don't think so -

23 rd. APil
색스피.어.

n. **party**   *n.* **present**   **to give** a present
                                        to get a present

Q. Do you like parties ?

Q. What do people do at parties ? *They usually do. dance*

Q. Did you have a party on your last birthday ? *NO. I. didn't*

Q. Did anyone sing 'Happy Birthday' ? *₩.00*

Q. When was the last time you went to a party ? *# I have Never gone to a party.*
Q. Was it good ?

Q. Do you like giving people presents ?

Q. What presents did you get on your last birthday ?

Q. Do you prefer giving presents or getting presents ? *I like more getting present then*

Q. What was the last present you bought ? *was giving # I bought for my*
Q. Who did you buy it for ? *for my ___*

Here are some irregular verbs.
keep   **kept**
sell   **sold**
put   **put**
give   **gave**
sleep   **slept**
mean   **meant**
run   **ran**

Q. What is the past of :
   a. keep ?   b. sell ?   c. put ?   d. give ?   e. sleep ?   f. run ?

v. **to start** + gerund   *v.* **to finish** + gerund
eg.   I **started** teaching English 5 years ago.
      This lesson **started** 5 minutes ago.
      We **finished** eating dinner and **started** watching television.
      I **finished** school when I was 18.

Q. When did you start studying English ?
Q. When did this lesson start ? *I. started. studying English. in ( ). ed*

Q. How old were you when you started school ? *10 m² when I was. started school*
Q. How old were you when you finished school ?

Q. When did I start teaching you English ? *you started teaching me. English me*

The verb **can** is irregular.

present	*past simple*
can / can't	**could / couldn't**

Q. Can you speak English ?

Q. Could you speak English when you were a child ?

Q. Can you usually understand me ?

Q. Could you understand me on your first day here ?

Q. Could you swim well when you were a child ?

v. to happen

We often use **happen** in questions.

eg.   What **happens** to people when they drink a lot ?

What **happened** at the end of the film ?

NB.   We don't say: At the end of the film happened ...

Q. What usually happens at the beginning of the lesson ?*

Q. What is happening now in this classroom ?

Q. What happens when people drink a lot of wine ?

Q. What tense do we use for an action that happens:

   a. in the past ?   b. now ?

Q. Did anything interesting happen yesterday ?

Unit 8

     v. **to get up**
           got up

Q. What time do you usually get up ? *I usually get up at 07:00.*
Q. What time did you get up this morning ? *I got up at 06:00 this morning.*

Q. Do you like getting up at 6 o'clock in the morning ? *I don't like getting up 6 o'clock.*

     v. **to go to bed**
           went to bed

Q. What time do you usually go to bed ? *I usually go to bed at*
Q. What time did you go to bed last night ? *I went to bed 12:00 last night*

Q. Do you ever read when you go to bed ? *yes I do sometimes.*

     adj. **early**   *adj.* **late**
Q. Did you go to bed late last night ? *Yes.*

Q. Do you prefer getting up early or late ?

Q. Do you prefer going to bed early or late ?

Q. What time did you get up this morning ? *I got up this morning.*
Q. Do you think that is early or late ?

Q. What time did you go to bed last night ? *I went to bed.*
Q. Do you think that is early or late ?

Q. Are the trains and buses ever late in this city ? *of cours*

Q. **Do you ever walk home from school ?**

Q. **Say something nice to him/her.**

Q. **Do you go to bed later at the weekends ?**

---

     v. **to be early / late <u>for</u>** something

Q. Are you ever late for school ? *Yes I I am sometime.*

Q. Are you ever early for school ?

Q. Are you ever late for work ?

Q. Were you late for school today ? *No I wasen't late for school today*
Q. Yesterday ?
Q. Last week ?

adj. **asleep**   adj. **awake**   *I sleep in a bed*

Q. Are you asleep or awake ? *I*
                                                (I am asleep (adj)
Q. Were you awake at 7 o'clock this morning ? *I wasn't* *I am sleeping*
Q. Were you asleep at 12 o'clock last night ? *awake at 7 o'clock this mo.*
Q. How do you know when someone is asleep ?
                                        eg: xo snoring

v. **to die**   adj. **dead**   adj. **alive**
   died

Q. Is Mozart alive or dead ?

Q. When did he die ?   *107 하*
A. Mozart died in 1791.

Q. Can you die from smoking ?

Q. Who died on 31st August, 1997 ?* ~~It~~ *Diana.*   *The _ of _*

Q. Is it good to be alive ?

adv. **still** *이너지 ... 기.*

Q. How old were you a year ago ? *I was.*
Q. Are you still ... ?

Q. Did you live with your parents when you *I was* were a child ?
Q. Are you still living with your parents now ? *I'm most still living.*
    I don't live with ~~you~~ my parents any more.
Q. Were you asleep at 6 o'clock this morning ? *yes I was asleep*
Q. Are you still asleep now ?
                                                No longer.
Q. Was the weather horrible or nice yesterday ?
Q. Is it still horrible/nice today ?

How far ?   adj. **near**
n. **metre**   n. **kilometre**

Q. Do you live near this school ?
Q. How far do you live from this school ? *How about*

Q. About how far is New York from here ?

Q. Is there a pub near this school ? *yes there*

Q. Are you sitting near the window ? *No.*

Q. About how far are you from the window ? *I am about* *m.*

prepositions of place

prep. **next to**   prep. **opposite***

prep. **in front of**   prep. **behind**

Q. What is opposite:
  a. this school ?   b. your house ?

Q. Am I standing in front of you or behind you ? *Your ar .*

Q. Is there a garden :
  a. in front of your house ?   b. behind your house ?

Q. Who is sitting next to you ?

Q. What is next to this school ?

adv. **nearly**   adv. **almost**

Nearly and **almost** mean the same thing.

  eg.   My brother is **nearly** 2 metres tall. (He is 1.98m tall.)
     It's **almost** Christmas! (It's the 23rd of December.)
     It's **nearly** 5 o'clock. (It's 4.57)

Q. When it's 11.29, what do we say ? *We say nearly 11.30*

Q. When it's 6.43, what do we say ?

Q. Is this book almost finished ? *≠ is'nt .*

Q. Are you nearly asleep ?

n. **future**   n. **tomorrow**

Yesterday is the past.
Today is the present.
Tomorrow is **the future**.

Q. Is yesterday the past ?

Q. Is today the present ?

Q. Is tomorrow the future ?

the future simple   will

We use **the future simple** for an action in the future.

will + infinitive   I will go - contraction = **I'll go** ...
will + not + infinitive I will not go - contraction = **I won't go** ...

  eg.   **I will** be 20 on 25th December.
     I'll go on holiday in July.
     I won't be here tomorrow.

Q. Will you come to the lesson tomorrow ?

Q. What time will you start studying tomorrow ?

Q. What time will you finish studying today ?

Q. Will you be awake at 9 o'clock this evening ?
Q. Will you still be awake at 12 o'clock ?

Q. Will I come to the lesson tomorrow ? - Ask.

> Because we don't always know what will happen in the future, we often use **I think + will**.
> eg. **I think I will** have chicken for dinner tonight.
> **I think the film will** be very good.

Q. What time do you think you will go to bed tonight ?

Q. What time do you think you will get up tomorrow ?

Q. What do you think you will do this weekend ?

Q. How many students do you think there will be here tomorrow ?

> *adj.* **next**
> We use **last** for the past : **last** week, **last** month, **last** year.
> We use **next** for the future : **next** week, **next** month, **next** year.

Q. What will next month be ?

Q. What will next year be ?

Q. What will the date be tomorrow ?

Q. Do you think you'll still be at this school next month ?
Q. Where do you think you'll live next year ?
Q. How old were you on your last birthday ?
Q. How old will you be on your next birthday ?

Q. How old was he/she on his/her last birthday ?
Q. How old will he/she be on his/her next birthday ? - Ask !

> *adj.* **rich**   *adj.* **poor**

Q. Give me an example of a very rich person.

Q. Are you rich ?

Q. Do you think you will be rich in the future ?

Q. Do you think there will always be rich people and poor people ?

Q. Do you think rich people are usually happier than poor people ?

adj. **famous**

Q. Give me an example of a famous person.

Q. Are famous people often rich ?

Q. Do you think you will be famous in the future ? *I think*

Q. Which famous person wrote, 'To be or not to be, that is the question.'

v. **to cross**   prep. **across** *I go across*
n. **bridge**

Q. Do you cross the street when you come to school ? *I'm cross the*

Q. Is there a river in this city ?
Q. About how many bridges are there across it ?

Q. Why is it sometimes difficult to cross the road ?

Q. Give me an example of a famous bridge ?

Q. What kind of things do bridges cross ?

n. **tunnel**   prep. **through**

Q. What kind of things do tunnels go under ?

Q. Do you travel through a tunnel when you come to school ?

Q. Who was the last person to come through that door ?

Q. Do you walk across a bridge or through a bridge ?

v. **to talk**   prep. **about**
to talk **to** someone   to talk **about** a subject
eg.   I **talked to** my mother on the phone yesterday.
My friend likes **talking about** football.

Q. Who am I talking to ?
? I am talkin to your
Q. Who do you talk to when you are sad ? *I talk.*

Q. Do you think men and women talk about the same things ? *I think*

Q. What kind of things do you talk to your friends about ?

Q. What kind of things do you talk to your parents about ?

Q. Talk about your country ?

n. **apostrophe**

1. We use an **apostrophe** with the possessive **'s**.
eg.   This is Andy**'s** book.
When the noun is plural, the apostrophe comes after the s:
eg.   The boy**s'** shirts were very dirty.
With irregular plurals (ie. plurals without s) the apostrophe comes before the s.
eg.   The children**'s** books were on the floor.

2. We use an **apostrophe** with contractions.
eg.   I ca**n't** speak French.
He**'s** got a new computer.
They did**n't** go on holiday last year.

3. We use an **apostrophe** when we talk about time in the future.
eg.   **In** 1 year**'s** time = 1 year in the future
In 2 years**'** time = 2 years in the future*
In 10 minute**s'** time = 10 minutes in the future*

Q.   How old are you ?
Q.   How old will you be in 10 years' time ?

Q.   What is today's date ?
Q.   What will the date be in 2 days' time ?

Q.   Do you think you'll still be at this school in a year's time ?

Q.   Do you think you will be rich in 10 years' time ?

adv. **soon**

He will be here **soon**.   (In about 5 minutes' time.)
I will go on holiday **soon**.   (In about two weeks' time.)
It will be my birthday **soon**. (In a month's time.)

Q.   Will you go on holiday soon ?
Q.   How soon ?

Q.   Will it be your birthday soon ?
Q.   How soon ?

Q.   Give me an example of something that you will do soon.

Q.   Give me an example of something that will happen soon.

Q.   Will you speak good English soon ?
Q.   How soon ?
A.   In about...

comparatives (2)

Remember : We use the letters 'er' to make a comparative with 1 syllable adjectives

adjective	comparative
big	**bigger**
small	**smaller**
nice	**nicer**

1. We use the letters 'er' to make a comparative with **2 syllable** adectives ending in **y**.

adjective	comparative
happy	**happier**
easy	**easier**
dirty	**dirtier**

2. For adjectives of two and three syllables, we add the words **more** or **less** to make the comparative :

adjective	comparative	comparative
famous	**more** famous **than**	**less** famous **than**
expensive	**more** expensive **than**	**less** expensive **than**
interesting	**more** interesting **than**	**less** interesting **than**
beautiful	**more** beautiful **than**	**less** beautiful **than**

eg.   Champagne is **more expensive than** wine.
I thought geography was **more interesting than** maths at school.

Q.   Give me an example of a famous writer from your country.
Q.   Do you think he/she is more famous than Shakespeare ?

Q.   What was your favourite subject at school ?
Q.   Did you think it was more interesting than English ? I .
        the -

Q.   Do you think your city is more beautiful than London ?

Q.   Do you think reading English is more difficult than writing English ?

Q.   Do you think food will be more expensive next year ?   *I don't think*

        I don't will be

Q.   **Where does the teacher usually stand ?**

Q.   **Do you think it will rain tomorrow ?**

Q.   **Do you go across a tunnel or through a tunnel ?**

> **subject + verb + object**
>
> *n.* **object**
> An English sentence usually has a **subject**, a **verb** and an **object**.
> eg.   Mozart wrote music.
>   My sister plays football.

John likes apples.

Q. Which word is :
   a. the subject ?   b. the verb ?   c. the object ?

Claire ate a banana.

Q. Which word is :
   a. the subject ?   b. the verb ?   c. the object ?

subject pronoun	object pronoun
I	me
you	you
he/she	him/her
it	it
we	us
you	you
they	them

Q. What are the subject pronouns ?

Q. What are the object pronouns ?

He knows me.

Q. Which word is :
   a. the subject pronoun ?   b. the object pronoun ?

She forgot him.

Q. Which word is :
   a. the subject pronoun ?   b. the object pronoun ?

They liked it.

Q. Which word is :
   a. the subject pronoun ?   b. the object pronoun ?

Q. What did you have for breakfast this morning ?
Q. Did you enjoy it ?

Q. Do you ever watch films on television ?
Q. Do you always like them ?

Q. Do you know him/her ?

Q. What is the object pronoun for :
   a. I   b. you   c. he   d. she   e. it   f. we   g. they ?

n. **the difference***   *prep.* **between**

Q. What is **the difference between** someone and something ?
A. We use someone for people and something for things.

Q. What is **the difference between** bad and badly ?
A. Bad is an adjective and badly is an adverb.

Q. What is the difference between I and me ?

Q. What is the difference between they and them ?

Q. What is the difference between I sit and I am sitting ?

Q. What is the difference between I am and I was ?

Q. What is the difference between a cupboard and a wardrobe ?

n. **place**

New York	**beach**
Australia	**restaurant**
kitchen	**street**

eg.   New York is a **place** in America.
A kitchen is a **place** to cook food in a house.

Q. Is New York a big place ?

Q. What is your favourite place for a holiday ?

Q. Are there any beautiful places in your country ?

Q. What kind of place is Australia ?

Q. Do you think London is an interesting place ?

Q. Do you know a good place to eat near here ?

v. **to come back**   *v.* **to go back**

Remember : we **come** *here* (the place where you are)
                    we **go** *there* (a different place)
We use **come back** when you come to a place you were before.
eg.   I will go on holiday tomorrow but I will **come back** here next Saturday.
We use **go back** when you go to a place you were before.
eg.   I went to France last year and I think I will **go back** there this summer.

Q. When will you go back to your country ?

Q. Do you think you will ever come back here ?

Q. Where did you go on holiday last year ?
Q. Do you think you'll you go back there ?

Q. Do you like this school ?
Q. Will you come back in the future ?

Q. Do you usually go back to a restaurant when the food was bad the first time ?

v. **to bring** (back)   *v.* **to take** (back)
       brought   took

Bring means to come here with something.
Take means to go there with something.
eg.   I always **bring** my book to the lesson.
       I always **take** my bag home after school.

Q.   What things do you always bring to school ?
Q.   Do you always take them home after the lesson ?

Q.   Do you ever bring food or drink to the classroom ?

Q.   What is the past simple of:
       a. to bring ?   b. to take ? *took*

Q.   What did you bring to school today ?

Q.   What things did you take on your last holiday ?

Q.   What kind of things do you take on a holiday :
       a. in the mountains ?   b. on the beach ?

Q.   Do you always remember to take your bag home with you ?
Q.   Did you take your bag home after the lesson yesterday ?

Q.   What will you take back to your country ?

Q.   **Where do you keep your glasses when you are not using them ?**

Q.   **What is the difference between a bowl and a plate ?**

Q.   **Give me an example of an interesting place in your country.**

Q.   **Do you ever forget to bring your book to school ?**

---

v. **to laugh**   *v.* **to cry**
       laughed   cried

Q.   What do children do when they are :
       a. very happy ?   b. very sad ?

Q.   Do people laugh a lot when they are drunk ?

Q.   When do babies cry ?

Q.   Do you think children laugh more than adults ?

Q.   Do people ever cry when they are happy ?

adj. **funny**   *n.* **actor**   *n.* **actress**

Q.   What do people do when they think something is very funny ?

Q.   Do you like funny films ?

Q. Give me an example of an actor/actress who is often in funny films.

Q. What kind of things do people laugh about ?

possessive adjectives	possessive pronouns
my	**mine**
your	**yours**
his	**his**
her	**hers**
our	**ours**
your	**yours**
their	**theirs**

Remember we use pronouns when we don't use a noun.
eg.   This is my **bag**.
        This is **mine**. (mine = my bag)
        His shoes are cleaner than **mine**. (mine = my shoes)
Q.   Whose book is that ?
A.   It's **hers**.
Q.   Whose dog is that ?
A.   It's **theirs**.

Q. Whose book is this ?

Q. Whose shoes are those ?

Q. Whose trousers are these ?

Q. Is that pen yours ?

Q. Are your shoes cleaner than mine ?

Q. Is my hair longer or shorter than yours ?

Q. Is your country bigger than theirs ?

Unit 9

verb forms

n. verb form   *n.* past participle

A verb form is the present, the past and the **past participle** of a verb.
The **past participle** of a regular verb is the same as the past simple.
So, the **verb form** of 'to use' is :

use	present
used	past simple
used	**past participle**

Q.   What is the verb form of :
a. to use ?   b. to like ?   c. to play ?   d. to walk ?

irregular verb forms

Some English verbs are irregular.
Here are some irregular verb forms.

present	past simple	past participle
have	had	**had**
know	knew	**known**
teach	taught	**taught**

Q.   What is the verb form of to have ?

Q.   What is the verb form of to know ?

Q.   What is the verb form of to teach ?

the present perfect (1)

We make the **present perfect** with the verb **to have** and **the past participle**:

I	have	taught	English	for	three	years.
subject +	to have +	past participle				

eg.   The present perfect of the verb to teach is :

I **have taught**	we **have taught**
you **have taught**	you **have taught**
he/ she **has taught**	they **have taught**

We often use the **present perfect** when an action starts in the past and is still happening in the present.
eg.   I started teaching English 3 years ago and I am still teaching English now.
        So, **I have taught** English for three years.

Q. How long have you known me ?
A. I have known you for ...

Q. Do you have a job?
Q. How long have you had your job ?

Q. When did you buy your book ?
Q. How long have you had it ?

Q. Who is your favourite actor ?
Q. How long have you liked him/her ?

Q. How long have I taught you English ?

---

been
The past participle of the verb to be is **been**.
So, the present perfect of the verb to be is :

I **have been**   we **have been**
you **have been**   you **have been**
he/she **has been**   they **have been**
it **has been**

Q. How long have you been in this city ?

Q. How long have you been in this classroom ?

Q. What is your father's/mother's job ?
Q. How long has he/she been a ... ?

Q. How long have I been a teacher ? - Ask me.

Q. How long has he/she been a student at this school ? - Ask.

prep. **for**   *prep.* **since**
We use **for** to say how long an action has happened.
eg.   I have taught English **for** three years.

We use **since** to say when an action started.
eg.   I have taught English **since** 1997.

Q. How long have you known me ?
Q. Since when ?

Q. How long have you been in this city ?
Q. Since when ?

Q. How long have you been at school today ? I have been
Q. Since what time ?

Q. Give me an example of the present perfect with since.

Here are some irregular verb forms:

present	past	past participle
write	wrote	**written**
read	read	**read***
make	made	**made**

Q. What is the verb form of :
   a. to write ?   b. to read ?   c. to make ?

---

present perfect (2)

We can use the present perfect to talk about the things we have done in our life.
eg.   I **have read** 'Romeo and Juliet'.
      I **have taught** English in France.

We often use the word **ever** to ask questions about people's lives.
The word **ever** means *'In your life'*.
We use **ever** for questions but **not** in answers.

eg.   Q.   Have you **ever** studied English history ?
      A.   Yes, I have studied English history. NOT ~~Yes I have ever...~~

We use **never** for negative answers.
eg.   Q.   Have you **ever** studied German ?
      A.   No, I have **never** studied German.

Q. Have you ever used a computer ?

Q. Have you ever lived in America ?

Q. Have you ever watched a French film ?

Q. Have you ever read an English newspaper ?

Q. Have you ever written a letter in English ?

Q. Have you ever made dinner for your family ?

Q. Have you ever had :
   a. an English breakfast ?   b. beer for breakfast ?   c. Indian food ?

v. **to meet** (someone)	*v.* **to see**
met	**saw**
met	**seen**

Q. What is the verb form of to meet ?
   The verb form of to meet is meet met met
Q. What is the verb form of to see ?

✓**Q.** When do people say when they meet for the first time ?

Q. When did you first meet me ?
   I did first meet you 1 month ago

Q. Have you ever met a famous person ?

Q. Have you ever seen a famous person ?

Q. What was the last film you saw ?

Q. Have you ever seen :
   a. an elephant ?   b. a spider that was bigger than your hand ?

Here are some more irregular verb forms.

present	past	past participle
forget	forgot	**forgotten**
drink	drank	**drunk**
buy	bought	**bought**

Q. What is the verb form of
   a. to forget   b. to drink   c. to buy

Q. Have you ever forgotten your mother's birthday ?

No. I have never forgotten my mother's b~

Q. Have you ever forgotten to bring your book to the lesson ?

No. I have never forgotten to bring ~

Q. Have you ever drunk Champagne ?

Q. Have you ever drunk Champagne for breakfast ?

✓*Q.* Have you ever drunk more than one bottle of wine ?

Q. Have you ever bought clothes from :
   a. a market ?   b. a very expensive shop ?

✓*Q.* Has anyone ever bought you something you didn't want ?

v. **to stay**   *n.* **hotel**   *v.* **to wait** (for)

✓*Q.* What kind of places do people stay in when they go on holiday ?

Q. When was the last time you stayed in a hotel ?   th   1 month ago   No votes

✗ *Q.* How long do you think you will stay in this city ?   for

Q. Have you ever stayed in an expensive hotel ?

Q. Do you like waiting ?

Q. What kind of things do people wait for ?   people wait for z te

Q. Have you ever waited more than an hour for a bus ?

Q. Have you ever waited for someone who didn't come ?   No. I have

v. **to try**

The verb to try has two meanings :

1. **try + infinitive**
   eg.   I **try** to get up early every morning but sometimes I can't.
         I can't always remember my students' names but I always **try**.*

Q. What am I trying to do ?*

Q. Have you ever tried to understand English radio ?

Q. Do you always try hard to answer my questions ?

Q. Have you ever tried to make bread ?

Q. Have you ever tried to stand on your head ?

Q. Has anyone ever tried to sell you something you didn't want ?
Q. Did you buy it ?

2. **try + noun/gerund** = to do something for the first time

Q. Do you like trying new things ?

Q. When was the first time you tried English food ?
Q. Did you like it ?

Q. Have you ever tried :
    a. snails ?   b. rabbit ?   c. horse meat ?

Q. Have you ever tried water-skiing ?
Q. Do you want to try it ?

Q. Is there anything you want to try ?

adj. **particular**   **particular time**

A **particular time** is *one* time in the past or the future :

an hour ago   in 2 weeks' time
last Tuesday   next Thursday
3rd January, 1995   4th of August, 2035
5 years ago   in 2 years' time

When we talk about a **particular time** in the past we use the **past simple**.

I **went** to Africa 2 years ago. - a particular time
I **ate** Chinese food last week. - a particular time
My mother **worked** in a shop in 1992. - a particular time
He **was** born on 28th of June, 1966. - a particular time

Answer these questions with a particular time in the past.

Q. When were you born ?

Q. When did Princess Diana die ?*

Q. When did you start school ?

Q. When was the first time you met me ?

Q. When did this lesson begin ?

Q. When was the last time you :
    a. went to the cinema ?   b. bought some new clothes ?   c. had foreign food ?

the present perfect and the past simple

1. We use the present perfect to talk about an action in the past but we do not say when it happened.

 eg. Q. **Have** you ever **lived** in America ?
 A. Yes, I **have lived** in America. (We **do not** say when it happened.)

2. We use the past simple when we talk about an action that happened at a **particular time** in the past.

 eg. Q. When **did** you live in America ?
 A. I **lived** in America **3 years ago**. (We say when it happened - at a particular time in the past.)

Q. Have you ever stayed in a very bad hotel ?
Q. Do you know when he/she stayed there ?*

Q. Have you ever had a big party for your birthday ?
Q. Do you know when he/she had the party ?*

Q. Have you ever stayed in Paris ?
Q. Do you know when he/she went there ?*

Q. Have you ever been very drunk ?
Q. When was the last time ?

Q. Have you ever waited for someone in the rain ?
Q. Do you know when that happened ?*

Q. Have you ever seen a famous person ?
Q. Who did you see ?
Q. Where did you see him/her ?
Q. When did you see him/her ?

Q. Ask him/her a question about his/her life with the present perfect.

Here are some more irregular verb forms.

present	past	past participle
eat	ate	**eaten**
sleep	slept	**slept**
get up	got up	**got up**

n. **midday**   *n.* **midnight**

Q. What is the verb form of :
 a. to eat ?   b. to sleep ?   c. to get up ?

Q. Have you ever eaten **frogs'** legs ?

Q. Have you ever slept on the floor ?

Q. Have you ever got up later than midday ?

Q. Do you usually go to bed before or after midnight ?

v. **to drive**
drove
driven

n. **lorry**

n. **van**

Q. What is the verb form of to drive ?

Q. Can you drive ?
Q. Have you got a car ?
Q. Have you ever driven :
a. a lorry ?   b. a van ?

Q. Have you ever driven a car very fast ?

Q. Have you ever driven on the left ?

v. **to ride**
rode
ridden

n. **a bicycle** (bike)
n. **a horse**
n. **a motorbike**

Q. What is the verb form of to ride ?

Q. Have you ever ridden :
a. a horse ?   b. a motorbike ?   c. an elephant ?

Q. How old were you when you first rode a bicycle ?

v. **to learn**
learnt
learnt*

Q. Have you learnt anything new today ?
Q. What have you learnt ?

Q. How old were you when you :
a. learnt to speak ?   b. learnt to write ?   c. learnt to ride a bike ?

Q. Have you ever tried to learn French ?
Q. Was it easy or difficult ?

v. **to fly**
flew
flown

n. **aeroplane** (plane)
n. **helicopter**
n. **bird**

Q. What is the verb form of to fly ?

Q. Did you fly to this country ?

Q. Have you ever flown in an aeroplane ?

Q. Have you ever flown in a helicopter ?

a cape

Q. Can birds fly ?

Q. At what time of day do birds sing ?

Q. What kind of birds do we eat ?

v. **to get**	*n.* **station***	*n.* **airport**	*n.* **port**
	n. **train**	*n.* **plane**	*n.* **boat**
	n. **bus**		

Q. Where do you get a train ?

Q. Where do you get a plane ?

Q. Where do you get a boat ?

Q. How can you get from an airport to the city ?

Q. What can you buy in an airport ?

v. **to travel**	*n.* **ticket**
	single / one way **standard**
	return **first class**

Q. Do you like travelling ?

Q. Which countries do you want to travel to in the future ?

Q. Do you usually buy a single or a return ticket when you travel abroad ?

Q. Have you ever travelled :
   a. by boat ?   b. by helicopter ?   c. first class ?

Q. Is it quicker to travel by boat or by plane ?

Q. Is it cheaper to travel first class or standard ?

Q. What kind of ticket do we buy when we want to go somewhere and come back ?

adj. **high**   *adj.* **low**
We use **high** and **low** for things, not people.

Q. What is the opposite of high ?

Q. What is the difference between :
   a. tall and high ?   b. short and low ?

Q. About how high does an aeroplane fly ? (10,000m)

Q. In which countries are there a lot of very high mountains ?

adj./n. **north**   n. **part** (of)
adj./n. **south**
adj./n. **east**
adj./n. **west**

eg.   Q.   Which **part of** your country are you from ?
        A.   I'm from **the north** / **south** / **east** / **west** of my country.
      NB.   We say : **in the north of ...**

Q.   What part of your country are you from ?

Q.   Are there any mountains in your country ?
Q.   In which part ?

Q.   Are there any beautiful places in your country ?
Q.   What part of your country are they in ?

Q.   Have you ever been to the north of Europe ?

Q.   Is the north of your country colder than the south of your country ?

n. **capital**

Q.   What is the capital of your country ?

Q.   What part of your country is the capital in ?

Q.   What is the capital of England ?
Q.   What part of the country is it in ?

n. **age**   at the **age** of 10
                    at 10

Q.   At what age do babies begin to talk ?

Q.   At what age did you start school ?

Q.   At what age can you drive in your country ?
Q.   Do you think we are about the same age ?

n. **size**

Q.   Have you got big feet ?
Q.   So, what size are your shoes ?

Q.   What size do you think my shoes are ?

Q.   Are we about the same size ?

n. **height**   *n.* **weight**

Q.   Do you know your weight in :
     a. kilograms ?   b. pounds ?

Q.   Do you know your height in :
     a. metres and centimetres ?   b. feet and inches ?

the same + noun + as

   eg.   Americans speak **the same language as** English people.
        I am about **the same height as** my brother.

Q.   Do you think you are about the same age as me ?
Q.   So are you older or younger than me ?

Q.   Is your city about the same size as London ?
Q.   So is it bigger or smaller than London ?

Q.   Is your bedroom about the same size as this classroom ?

Q.   Are you the same height now as when you were 15 ?

Q.   Are you about the same height as anyone here ?

---

to go and **to be** in the **present perfect**

Study these two sentences :
My mother **has been** to Paris. (My mother went to Paris and she came back.)
My mother **has gone** to Paris. (My mother went to Paris and she hasn't come back, but she is <u>still</u> there.)

My friend <u>has been</u> to New York.

went

Q.   Did my friend go to New York ?

Q.   Has my friend come back here ?
Q.   So is my friend still in New York ?   *any more*

My friend <u>has gone</u> to New York.

went

Q.   Did my friend go to New York ?

Q.   Has my friend come back ?
Q.   So is my friend still in New York ?

Q.   Is my friend here ?
Q.   Why not ?

superlatives

Adjectives of one syllable or two syllables ending in Y.
Remember :   we make a comparative by adding the letters - **er** to an adjective.
We make a superlative with **the** and by adding the letters - **est** to an adjective.
the + adjective - **est**

adjective -	London is **big**.
comparative -	London is **bigger than** Paris.
superlative -	London is **the biggest** city in Europe.

adjective -	My grandmother is **old**.
comparative -	My grandmother is **older than** me.
superlative -	My grandmother is **the oldest** person in my family.

Q.   What is the biggest city in your country ?

Q.   Is it the capital ?

Q.   Who is the tallest person in your family ?

Q.   Who is the oldest :
   a. man in your family ?   b. woman in your family ?
   c. child in your family ?   d. person in this class ?

Q.   Which is the nearest station to :
   a. your house ?   b. this school ?

Q.   Which was the easiest subject you studied at school ?

n. **the world**   *n.* **continent**
There are six **continents** in the world.

Asia	Europe	North America
South America	Africa	Australasia

Q.   How many continents are there in the world ?

Q.   Which continent are you from ?

Q.   What is the biggest country in the world ?

Q.   What is the longest river :
   a. in your country ?   b. in the world ?

Q.   What is the highest mountain :
   a. in your country ?   b. in the world ?

Here are some more irregular verb forms.

present	past	past participle
give	gave	**given**
run	ran	**run**
bring	brought	**brought**
take	took	**taken**

Q.   Have you ever given flowers to anyone ?
Q.   Who did you give them to and why ?

Q.   Have you ever given money to someone in the street ?

Q.   Have you ever run for a bus ?

Q.   Have you ever brought :
       a. food to the classroom ?   b. a friend to the school ?

Q.   Have you ever taken clothes back to a shop because you didn't like them ?

---

superlatives (2)
Adjectives with two or more syllables.
Remember :   we make a comparative with the words 'more' or 'less'.
                     We make a superlative with the word **most.**

adjective -   I think geography is very **interesting.**
comparative -   I think geography is **more interesting than** history.
superlative -   Geography was **the most interesting** subject I studied at school.

Q.   What was the most interesting subject you studied at school ?
         Math was the most interestin subject I studied at school
Q.   What was the most boring subject you studied at school ?
         Chemistry was. I
Q.   What is the most beautiful part of your country ?
         mauntin was.
Q.   Who do you think is the most beautiful actress in the world ?
         I think ___ is the
Q.   Who do you think is the most famous person in your country ?

          n. **fact**   *n.* **opinion**
          London is in the south of England. = **fact**
          London is the most interesting city in Europe. = **opinion**

Q.   Listen to these sentences and say '**fact**' or '**opinion**'.

1.   Brazil is a big country.
2.   Britain is a beautiful country.
3.   Pasta is nice with cheese.
4.   Pasta comes from Italy.
5.   Coffee is horrible.
6.   Champagne is more expensive than milk.
7.   Russia is the biggest country in the world.
8.   English grammar is very interesting.

          v. **to think**   *n.* **brain**
               thought
               thought
          The verb **to think** has two meanings:
          1.   To use your brain.

Q.   Where is your brain ?

Q. Do you think hard when you :
   a. study English ?
   b. watch English television ?
   c. watch television in your country ?

2.   To give your opinion about something.
      We often say **"I think that"** for an opinion.
 eg.   I **think that** Italian food is very nice.
       He **thinks that** this country is beautiful.

Q. Do you think that your country is very beautiful ?

Q. Do you think that the food in your country is nicer than English food ?

Q. Who do you think is the most famous English person ?

---

irregular comparatives and **superlatives**

adjective	comparative	superlative
good	**better than**	**the best**
bad	**worse than**	**the worst**

Q. Can I speak English better than you ?

Q. Can you speak your language better than me ?

Q. Are England better at football than your country ?

Q. Do you think that English food is better or worse than the food from your country ?

Q. Do you think English weather is better or worse than the weather in your country ?

Q. What was your best subject at school ?
Q. What was your worst subject at school ?

Q. What is the best present you have ever had ?

Q. Who do you think is the best :
   a. writer from your country ?   b. student in the class ?   c. actress in the world ?

Q. What kind of clothes are best for :
   a. playing football ?   b. skiing ?
   c. a holiday on the beach ?   d. working in the garden ?   overalls

Q. Who was your best friend at school ?
Q. Are they still your best friend ?

Here are some more irregular verb forms.

present	past simple	past participle
hear	heard	**heard**
sing	sang	**sung**
stand	stood	**stood**

The Shawshank Redeuption
& Schindler's List.

Q. What is the verb form of :
    a. to hear ?   b. to sing ?   c. to stand ?

Q. Have you ever heard the birds singing in the morning ?

Q. Have you ever heard anyone singing in the bath ?

Q. Have you ever sung at a party ?

Q. Have you ever stood up for a long time in a train or a bus ?

---

superlatives and **the present perfect**

We often use superlatives with the present perfect when we talk about our life and opinions.

eg.   London isn't <u>the biggest</u> city in the world but it is <u>the biggest</u> city I **have ever been** to.

NB. We usually use **ever** in these sentences in the negative and the positive.

Q. What is the best film you have ever seen ?

Q. What is the most interesting/boring subject you have ever studied ?

Q. What is the most expensive city you have ever been to ?

Q. What is the most difficult subject you have ever studied ?

Q. What is the best place you have ever been to on holiday ?   *was*

math isn't the most interesting but it is interesting subject
subject.   I have ever.
*   studied*

Unit 10

adj. **sure**   *v.* **to be sure** (about something)

I am sure = I **know** something is a fact.

eg.   I **am sure** that London is the capital of England.

Q.   What is the capital of England ?
Q.   Are you sure ?

Q.   What is the capital of America ?
Q.   Are you sure ?

NB. When people aren't sure about something they often use 'I think'.

eg.   **I'm not sure** but I **think** Berlin is the capital of Germany.
       I **think** you are younger than me but **I'm not sure**.

Q.   How old do you think I am ?
Q.   Are you sure ?

Q.   What is the biggest city in the world ?
Q.   Are you sure ?

Q.   Who was the first European to go to America ?   christopher colombus
Q.   Are you sure ?

콜롬버스

adv. **probably** = 80 %

When you say something will **probably** happen, you think it will happen but you are *not* sure.

eg.   I think it will **probably** rain later.
       She thinks she will **probably** come to the party, but she isn't sure.

Answer these questions using probably.
Q.   Do you think you will get richer in the future ?
Q.   Are you sure ?

Q.   Do you think you will use English in your job ?

Q.   Do you think plane tickets will get more expensive in the future ?

Q.   Give me an example of a sentence using probably.

v. **to smoke**   *n.* **smoking**
n. **cigarette**   *n.* **cigar**   *n.* **packet** (of cigarettes)

Q.   Do you smoke ?
Q.   How many cigarettes have you smoked today ?*

Q. Have you ever smoked a cigar ?

Q. Are cigarettes more expensive in England than in your country ?

Q. Have you ever smoked more than a packet of cigarettes in one day ?

adj. **healthy**   *adj.* **unhealthy**

Q. Is smoking healthy ?

Q. What kind of food is healthy ?

Q. Do you think that the food in your country is healthier than English food ?

adj. **fresh** (fruit and vegetables)   *adj.* **frozen**

Q. Where do you buy your fresh fruit and vegetables ?   *ge*

Q. Where do you keep frozen food ?   *freezer*

Q. Which is healthier, fresh or frozen food ?

n. **park**   *n.* **theatre**   *n.* **play**

Q. Are there any parks in your city ?

Q. Do you like walking in the park on a sunny day ?

Q. Do you walk through a park when you come to school ?

Q. Where do we go to see a play ?   *To a theatre.*

Q. Give me an example of a famous play.

Q. Do you often go to the theatre ?

Q. Have you been to the theatre in this city ?
Q. What play did you see ?   *The phantom of the opea*

n. **air**   *n.* **the countryside**   *to breathe*

Q. Are you from a city or the countryside ?

Q. Do you know anyone who lives in the coutryside ?
Q. Who ?

Q. Is the air fresher in the city or the countryside ?

Q. Do you think that life in the city is better or worse than in the countryside ?

n. **town**   *n.* **village**
A **town** is smaller than a city.
A **village** is smaller than a town.

Q.   Were you born in a city, a town or a village ?

Q.   Is life healthier in a city or a village ?

n. **farm**
n. **field**   *n.* **grass**   *n.* **cow**   *n.* **sheep**

Q.   Have you ever been to a farm ?
Q.   What kind of animals did you see there ? *saw*

✓*Q.*   What do cows and sheep eat ?

Q.   Where do we keep cows and sheep ?   *Stock.farm*

adj. **dangerous** *rattle snake*   *adj.* **safe**
eg.   A policeman's job is often **dangerous**.
        Trains are **safer** than cars.

Q.   Is it safe to smoke cigarettes ?

Q.   Is your city a safe place to live ?

Q.   Is it safer to travel by plane or by train ?

Q.   Give me an example of a dangerous animal ?

Q.   What do you think is the most dangerous animal in your country ?   *snake (~~snake~~)*
        I. think. snake .is the

n. **seat belt**   *n.* **helmet**

Q.   Do you always wear a seat belt when you travel by car ?

Q.   What do people wear on their head when they ride a motorbike ?
Q.   Have you ever ridden a motorbike without a helmet ?

Q.   Do you think it is safe to ride a motorbike without a helmet ?

v. **to choose**   *n.* **choice**
    chose
    chosen
When we **choose** something we take one thing we prefer from different things.
eg.   People often **choose** a hot, sunny place for a holiday.
When you buy a new car you usually have a **choice** of colours.

Q.   Why did you choose this school ?

Q.   When you were a child did you choose *choose* your clothes or did your parents choose them ?

Q.   Do you always try hard to choose good presents for your friends ?

Q.   What kind of place do you usually choose for your summer holiday ?

Q. When you go clothes shopping do you usually choose what you want quickly ?

what I want quickly when I go.

Q. When you have a choice of drinks with dinner, what do you usually choose ?

Q. When you want to learn a foreign language, do you think English is the best choice ?

I.

> *adj.* **important**
> eg.   The President is the most **important** person in the USA.

Q. Is it important for you to learn English ?

Q. Why ?

Q. Do you think people are more important than animals ?

animals + people are equally important

Q. Do you think it is important to choose a good school for your children ?

Q. Are your friends important to you ?

Q. Who is the most important person in your life ? *is.*

people choose

Q. What kind of important choices do people make in their lives ?

my family Job.

who to marry
what job to hav
where to live
how many ch

> *[nes-i-seri]*
> *adj.* **necessary**   *v.* **to be necessary** to do something
> When something **is necessary** it is very important to do it.
> eg.   Warm clothes **are necessary** in winter.
>   A helmet **is necessary** when you ride a motorbike.
>   It **is necessary to** boil water to make tea ?
>   It **is not necessary to** cook carrots before eating them.

Q. Is it necessary to cook chicken before eating it ?

Q. Is it necessary to boil water to make tea ?

Q. Are warm clothes necessary when you go for a holiday on a beach ?

are it

Q. Is it necessary to wear a helmet when you ride a motorbike in your country ?

Q. What kind of things are necessary for a good party ?

Q. Do you think it is necessary to :
a. eat meat to be healthy ?   b. be rich to be happy ?

> *v.* **to have to**
>   had to
> We use **have to** when it is necessary to do something because we <u>do not</u> have a choice.
> eg.   I **have to** get up early because I start work at 8 o'clock.
>   My mother **has to** wear glasses when she reads because she can't see well.
>   I **had to** get a visa before I went to the USA last year.

Q. Do you have to speak English in the lesson ?

Q. Do you have to think hard when you speak English ?

Q. Do you know anyone who has to get up very early in the morning ?

Q. Why do they have to get up early ?

Q.   Do you have to wear glasses :
       a. to read ?   b. to watch television ?   c. to drive ?

Q.   What subjects do children have to study at school in your country ?
Q.   Which subjects can you choose ?

Q.   Do you have to get a visa to travel to the USA ?

Q.   Have you ever had to :
       a. live with someone you didn't like ?   b. walk home in the rain ?

Q.   Do you have to drive on the left or the right in your country ?

Negative of have to = **don't have to**
We use **don't have to** when it isn't necessary to do something because we have a choice.
eg.   I **don't have to** get up early at the weekend.
       English people **don't have to** get a visa to go to France.
       My mother **has to** wear glasses to drive but she **doesn't have to** wear glasses
       to read.

Q.   Do you have to eat meat to be healthy ?

Q.   Do French people have to get a visa to come to this country ?

Q.   Do you have to cook fish before eating it ?

Q.   Do you have to get up early in the morning at the weekend ?

Q.   Do children in your country have to study :
       a. English ?   b. French ?   c. Russian ?

Q.   Do you have to go to a very expensive restaurant to eat nice food ?

Q.   Make a sentence with :
       a. have to.   b. don't have to.

another = an + other (singular)   **other** (for plurals)
We use **other** and **another** when we talk about more of the same thing.
We usually use **another** with singular nouns and **other** with plural nouns.

another :   My rich uncle has bought **another** Rolls Royce.
                Do you want **another** cup of coffee.
other :   There are a lot of English-speaking countries, Britain is one and
                some **others** are the USA, Canada and Australia.
                I have two sisters, one is older than me and the **other** is younger.

NB. We use **more** with uncountable nouns.
eg.   Do you want **another** cup of coffee ?
                Do you want **more** coffee ?

Q.   Is there another language school in this street ?

Q.   Have you ever studied another foreign language ?
Q.   Which one ?

Q.   Give me an example of an adjective.
Q.   Give me another example.

Q. Give me an example of an English-speaking country.
Q. Give me another one.

Q. What is my name ?
Q. What are the names of your other teachers ?

Q. What nationality is he/she ?
Q. Are there any other ... students at this school ?

Q. Are there any other countries where they speak your language ?

v. **to get + adjective**   *adj.* **drunk**   *adj.* **sleepy**   *adj.* **angry**
People **get tired** when they work hard
People **get drunk** when they drink a lot.

Q. What happens when people drink a lot of beer ?   *they get drunk*

Q. What happens to people when they work very hard ?

Q. Do you get cold when you swim in the sea ?

Q. Do you get sleepy in the classroom ?

Q. What do you do when you :
   a. get hungry ?   b. get thirsty ?   c. get tired ?   *have a rest*
                                                                      + take a nap
Q. In what month does it get cold in your country ?
                                                                to have forty winks.
Q. Do you get angry easily ?

Q. Do you get angry when you have to wait a long time for someone ?

until (till)

1.   We use **until** to say what time an action finishes.
         eg.   I watched television **until** midnight.
               I will be here **until** 7 o'clock.
2.   We use **until** when we finish doing an action because of another action.
         eg.   We played tennis **until** it started raining.
               I studied English **until** I got tired.

Q. What did you do last night ?
Q. Until when ?

Q. Will you be here until the school closes ?   *No. I won't*

Q. Until what age do children have to stay at school in your country ?

Q. Have you ever been at a party until 6 o'clock in the morning ?

Q. Have you ever laughed until you cried ?

Q. Have you ever studied until you were very tired ?

enough   not enough

When you have **enough**, you have what is necessary.
When you **don't** have **enough**, you have less than is necessary.

1. We use **enough** before a noun :
eg.   There are **enough** chairs for 10 students in this classroom.
        I **don't** have **enough** money to go on holiday this summer.

Q. Is £1 enough for a cup of coffee in a cafe ?

Q. Do you think there are enough parks in your city ?

Q. Are there enough chairs for twenty students in this room ?

Q. Have you got enough money to buy :
  a. a pair of jeans ?   b. a bicycle ?   c. a house ?

Q. Do you know enough English to :
  a. write a short letter ? b. read a newspaper ?   c. write a book ?

2. We use **enough** after an adjective or an adverb.

Q. Is the weather warm enough to go to the beach ?

Q. Is your English good enough to be a teacher ?

Q. Is this classroom big enough for :
  a. 10 students ?   b. 20 students ?

Q. Are you old enough to drive a car ?

Q. Can you speak English well enough to :
  a. get a job in England ?   b. be an English teacher ?

v. **to touch**   *v.* **to carry**   *adj.* **strong**

Q. What part of my face am I touching ?

Q. Can you touch your toes ?

Q. What kind of animals do we use to carry people and things ?

Q. Are adults usually stronger than children ?

Q. Do you have to be strong to carry :
  a. a television ?   b. this book ?

Q. Are you strong enough to carry this table ?

Q. Are you tall enough to touch the ceiling ?

Q. Do you ever have to carry heavy shopping home ?

too   **too many**
               too much

We use **too much** and **too many** to say that there is more than necessary and this is a bad thing.

We use **too many** for countable nouns.

We use **too much** for uncountable nouns.

eg.   There are **too many** cars in this city.
       I think the Queen **has too** much money.

Q.   Are there a lot of cars in this city ?
Q.   Are there too many cars in this city ?

Q.   Are there a lot of beautiful beaches in your country ?
Q.   Are there too many ? *

Q.   Is it healthy to :
       a. drink too much beer ?   b. eat too much food ?

Q.   Are there ever too many people on the trains and buses ?

Q.   Do you know anyone who :
       a. drinks too much ?   b. smokes too much ?

too + adjective

We use **too + adjective** when there is more than is necessary and this is a bad thing.

eg.   I couldn't understand the book, it was **too** difficult.
       This coffee is **too hot** to drink. (I can't drink it because it is very hot.)

NB.   Paris is **very** beautiful. - right!
       Paris is **too** beautiful - wrong! This means we don't like Paris *because* it is beautiful.

Q.   Is it too cold to swim in the sea in winter ?

Q.   Do you think people can be too old to learn a foreign language ?

Q.   Are children too young to get married ?

Q.   Have you ever woken up too late to come to school ?

Q.   Have you ever tried reading a book that was too boring to finish ?

Q.   Do you think 16 is old enough to :
       a. ride a motorbike ?   b. drive a car ?   c. get married ? *

Q.   Are you too young to get married ?

Q.   Have you ever been too ill to come to school ?

Q.   **What kind of things can you see in the countryside ?**

Q.   **Who do you have to buy presents for at Christmas ?**

Q.   **Have you tried another English school ?**

Q.   **Do English people always speak slowly enough for you to understand ?**

© *Avalon Book Company Ltd., 1999*

if
1. Talking about the present.   **If + present + present**
We use **if** with the **present** to say an action generally happens because of another action.
eg.   **If** I **don't** sleep enough I **get** very tired.
I get very drunk **if** I **drink** a lot of wine.

Q.   If you don't sleep enough, do you get tired ?

Q.   Do you get hungry if you don't eat enough ?   *Yes I got hangry.*

Q.   Do you get drunk if you drink more than two glasses of wine ?

Q.   Can you sit down if there are a lot of people on the bus ?   *No.*

Q.   Do you always take a camera if you go on holiday ?

Q.   If the weather is nice, do you ever go to the park ?

2. Talking about the future.   **If + present + future**
We use **if** with the future when we think that an action will happen in the future **because of** another action.
We are not sure the action will happen but we think it will probably happen.
eg.   **If** I **study** hard I **will** learn English well.
If I **go** on holiday next year, I **will** go in June.

Q.   If you go on holiday this/next year, where will you go ?

Q.   If you study hard will you learn English well ?

Q.   If it is hot and sunny this weekend, what will you do ?
Q.   Will you still do that if the weather is horrible ?

Q.   Will you be sleepy in the morning if you go to bed very late tonight, ?

Q.   If you drink a lot of wine, what will probably happen ?   *get drunk to pass out*

Q.   If you see me in the street, will you say hello to me ?

Q.   Will you be happy or sad if you don't get any presents for your birthday ?

v. **to pay**	n. **bank**	n. **account**	n. **cheque**
paid	n. **cash**	n. **credit card**	n. **cashpoint**
paid			

Q.   Do you have a bank account ?
Q.   With which bank ?

Q.   How much cash do you usually keep in your wallet ?

Q.   If you buy something expensive, do you usually pay by cash, cheque or credit card ?

Q. Where can you get cash if the bank is closed ?

Q. What do have to remember when you use a cashpoint ?   *Pin No*

Q. How much did you pay for your bag/shoes/jacket ?

Q. Have you ever paid more than £100 for a pair of shoes ?

Q. Do you think it is dangerous to use a cashpoint at night ?

> *v.* **to lose**   *v.* **to find**
>   lost   found
>   lost   found

Q. What kind of things do people often lose ?

Q. Have you ever found any money in the street ?
Q. How much did you find ?

Q. What do you have to do if you lose your credit card ?   *locksmith.*

Q. How can you get in your house if you lose your keys ?

Q. Is it difficult to find a good job ?

Q. Have you ever lost something important ?

---

present perfect (3)
When someone asks a question in the present perfect we can use the past simple in the answer if we want to say the action happened at a particular time in the past.
eg.   Q.   Have you ever been to Russia ?
      A.   Yes, I **went** there **three years ago**.
      Q.   Have you ever met a famous person ?
      A.   Yes, I **met** the President **last week**.

Answer these questions with the past simple.

Q. Have you ever :
  a. lost your keys ?   b. eaten Indian food ?
  c. read an English book ?   d. had dinner in an expensive restaurant ?

> *n.* **company**   *v.* **to work for** (a company)
> *n.* **office**   *n.* **factory**

Q. What company do I work for ?

Q. What famous companies make :
  a. cars ?   b. computers ?   c. drinks ?

Q. What kind of things do people make in factories ?

Q. Does your mother/father have a job ?
Q. Which company does he/she work for and where does he/she work ?

Q. Do you think it is better to work :
  a. for a big or a small company ?   b. in a factory or an office ?

adj. **ill**   *n.* **illness**   *n.* **a cold**   *n.* **the flu**

n. **day off**   **take a** day off

Q. Have you ever been too ill to come to school ?
Q. So what did you do ?

Q. What illnesses have you had ?

Q. Which is worse, a cold or the flu ?

Q. Have you ever taken a day off work/school because you were very tired ?

Q. How many days off school have you taken this month ?

Q. Do you always stay at home if you are ill ?

v. **to cough**   *v.* **to sneeze**   *v.* **to yawn**

Q. Do people who smoke cough a lot ?

Q. What happens when you have a cold ?

Q. What do English people say when someone sneezes ?
Q. What do people say in your country ?

Q. Why do people yawn ?

adj. **polite**   *adj.* **rude**

Q. What words do we use to be polite ?

Q. Do you ever yawn when someone is talking to you ?
Q. Why not ?

Q. Has anyone been rude to you today ?

Q. Do you get angry if people are rude to you ?

all   every

All and **every** mean the same thing BUT :
1.   We use **all** with **plural** and **uncountable** nouns.
eg.   **All** my **friends** came to my party.
        Andy ate **all** the **food** at the party.

Q. Do you know all the students in this classroom ?

Q. Do you keep all your money in your pocket ?

Q. Do you know all the letters of the alphabet ?

2.   We use **every** with **singular** nouns -
eg.   **Every** country has a flag.

Q. Do you know every student in this school ?

Q. Do you come to school every day ?

Q. Does every house have a swimming pool in your country ?

all day = all the time during the day
every day = all the days of the week

Q. Have you ever watched TV all day ?
Q. Do you watch television every day ?

Q. Do you go on holiday all year ?
Q. Do you go on holiday every year ?

Q. If you are ill, do you stay in bed all day ?

Q. What kind of things do we do every day ?

Q. Is it hot all year in your country ?

    v. **to leave**   v. **to arrive**
         left
         left
to leave has two meanings :
1. to go out (of a place)
    to arrive is the opposite.
eg. I **leave** home at 8 o'clock every morning and arrive at work at about 9 o'clock.
     The train **left** the station twenty minutes ago.

Q. What time did you leave home today ?
Q. What time did you arrive here ?

Q. Do trains and buses sometimes arrive late ?

Q. What was the last thing you did before leaving home this morning ?

Q. At what age do children usually leave school in your country ?

Q. Have you ever left the cinema before the film finished ?
Q. Why ? It was boring

2. forget to take something/put something somewhere
eg. I **left** my umbrella on the train.
     I will **leave** the bottle of Champagne in the fridge until it is cold.

Q. Have you ever left anything on the train/bus ?

Q. Have you ever gone out and left your keys at home ?

Q. Do you ever leave dirty clothes on your bedroom floor ?

Q. Do you leave your bag in the classroom between lessons ?

both

We use **all** for more than two things.

For two things we use **both**.

eg.   Japan and Korea are **both** Asian countries.

Both my sisters are married. (So, you know I have two.)

Q.   Are both your feet on the floor ?

Q.   Are France and England both European countries ?

Q.   Do we both speak the same language :
   a. generally ?   b. in the lesson ?

Q.   Are you both from the same country ?

Q.   Are both of those books the same ?

n. **church**   *n.* **library**

Q.   Does every town have a church in your country ?

Q.   Do you go to church every Sunday ?

Q.   Does your town have a library ?

Q.   What do people use a library for ?

Q.   Do you think old churches are more beautiful than new ones ?

n. **furniture**

   n. **sofa**   *n.* **chest of drawers**   *adj.* **comfortable***

   n. **armchair**   *n.* **coffee table**   *adj.* **uncomfortable***

Bed, **table** and **chair** are all examples of **furniture**.

Furniture is an uncountable noun.

Q.   What furniture can you see in this room ?

Q.   What kind of furniture do you have in your living room ?

Q.   Where do you keep your coats and jackets ?

Q.   Is the furniture comfortable in your house ?

Q.   Have you ever slept in an uncomfortable bed ?

Q.   How many syllables are there in the word comfortable ?

Comf- ta- ble

Q.   **Are all English teachers from England ?**
Q.   **What other countries are they sometimes from ?**

Q.   **Have you ever danced all night ?**

Q.   **Have you ever left your bag in a shop or pub ?**
Q.   **Did you go back and try to find it ?**

Q.   **Give me an example of furniture :**
   a. we sit on ?   b. we sleep in ?   c. we keep things in ?

---

everyone   everything   everywhere

everyone means <u>all people</u>
everything means <u>all things</u>
everywhere means <u>all places</u>
NB. **Everyone**, **everything** and **everywhere** are <u>all</u> singular.

Q. Do you know everyone in this class ?

Q. Have you met everyone in this school ?

Q. Can you remember everything you learnt at school ?

Q. Do people eat the same food everywhere in the world ?

Q. Is there enough food for everyone in the world ?

Q. Do people drive on the right everywhere in the world ?

Q. Does everyone speak the same language :
    a. in your country ?   b. in America ?

Q. Have you got enough money to buy everything you want ?

   v. **to stop** + gerund
       stopped*
       stopped
To stop has two meanings :   a. the opposite of **start**
                      b. the opposite of **go**
eg.   I **stopped** smoking two weeks ago.
      Cars have to **stop** at a red light.

Q. What do cars have to do when a light is:
    a. red ?   b. green ?

Q. Is it easy to stop smoking ?

Q. Is there anything you did when you were a child that you have stopped doing now ?

Q. What are the two opposites of the verb to stop ?*

Q. Have you ever stopped speaking to someone because you were angry with them ?

   adj./ adv. **only**
   eg.   This is the **only** school in this street.
       We **only** teach English at this school.

Q. Is that the only door in this classroom ?

Q. Are you the only man/woman/student in this class ?

Q. Is English the only foreign language you speak ?

Q. Give me an example of something you only do when you are on holiday.

Q. What can we only see at night?

Q. What kind of animals only live in water?

would

We use **will** to make the future tense.
We use **would** to make the **conditional** tense.

eg. I **would** like to be rich.
It **would** be difficult to learn English without a book.
I **would** like to win the lottery.

Q. Would you like to be very, very rich ?

Q. Would you like to live in another country ?
Q. Which one ?

Q. Would you ever try :
a. beer for breakfast ?　　　b. frogs' legs ?

Q. How many children would you like to have ?

Q. Would you be happy working in a factory ?

Q. Is there anything you would like to stop doing ?

NB. We can also use **would** to be polite when we ask people questions.
eg. What **would** you like to drink ?
I **would** like a coffee please.
Would you open the window please ?

Q. Ask him / her a polite question using would.

Q. Are the chairs here more comfortable than your chairs at home ?

Q. Do you think it is rude to put your feet on a table ?

Q. Are jeans comfortable to wear ?

---

adv. **again**

If we do something **again**, we do it another time.
eg. I have been to Africa and I would like to go there **again**.
I stopped smoking six months ago, but now I have started **again**.

Q. Would you like to study the beginning of this book again ?

Q. Are there any places that you would never go to again ?

Q. Have you ever been to another country ?
Q. Would you like to go there again ?

Q. Would you like to be a child/teenager again ?

Q. Is there anything you did in the past that you would like to do again ?

the future intention - going to

(to be) **going to + infinitive**
We use **going to** when we say what we want to do in the future.
eg.   I am **going to** have a big party next weekend.
My father is ill so he is **going to** see the doctor tomorrow.

Q.   What are you going to have for dinner tonight ?

Q.   Are you going to study at home tonight ?

Q.   Are you going to get up early tomorrow ?

Q.   What are going to do on your next birthday ?

Q.   Are you going to meet your friends after school ?
Q.   Where are you going to meet them ?

Q.   What are you going to do after the lesson ?

Q.   What kind of job are you going to get when you go back to your country ?

Q.   What book are we going to study next ?

Irregular Verbs

infinitive	simple past	past participle
be	was, were	been
be born	was born	been born
begin	began	begun
bring	brought	brought
buy	bought	bought
choose	chose	chosen
come	came	come
come back	came back	come back
do	did	done
drink	drank	drunk
drive	drove	driven
eat	ate	eaten
find	found	found
fly	flew	flown
forget	forgot	forgotten
get	got	got
get up	got up	got up
give	gave	given
go	went	gone
go back	went back	gone back
have	had	had
have to	had to	had to
hear	heard	heard
learn	learnt	learnt
leave	left	left
mean	meant	meant
pay	paid	paid
put	put	put
read	read	read
ride	rode	ridden
run	ran	run
see	saw	seen
sell	sold	sold
sing	sang	sung
sit	sat	sat
stand	stood	stood
stand up	stood up	stood up
swim	swam	swum
take	took	taken
think	thought	thought
wear	wore	worn
write	wrote	written

Unit 1

A.   to be

1.   I ..… a student.

2.   You ..… a teacher.

3.   He ..… a man.

4.   She ..… a woman.

5.   It ..… a pencil.

6.   We ..… in the classroom.

7.   They ..… chairs.

B.   in / on

1.   The picture is ..…...... the wall.

2.   The students are ..…...... the classroom.

3.   The light is ..…....… the ceiling.

4.   The table is ..…...... the floor.

5.   5. We are ..…....… the classroom.

C.   there is / there are

1.   There ..…....… a table in the classroom.

2.   There ..…...... 12 chairs in the classroom.

3.   There ..…....… 4 pictures on the wall.

4.   There ..…....… one teacher in the classroom.

5.   There ..…...... two doors.

D.   how many ?

1.   How many chairs are there in the classroom ?

        There ....

2.   How many teachers are there in the classroom ?

        There ....

3.   How many students are there in the classroom ?

        There ....

4.   How many pictures are there on the wall ?

      There ....

E.   to be - negative or positive

1.   Are you a student ?   ....

2.   Are you a teacher ?   ....

3.   Is the light on the wall ?   ....

4.   Is your book on the floor ?   ....

5.   Is the teacher a man ?   ....

F.   There is / there are - negative or positive

1.   Is there a table in the classroom ?

      ....

2.   Is there a picture on the window ?

      ....

3.   Are there two teachers in the classroom ?

      ....

4.   Is there a book on your table ?

      ....

5.   Are there ten pictures on the walls ?

      ....

G.   a / the / in / on / is / are / there / her

1. His name .... John.   2. He is .... student.

3. His teacher .... a woman.   4. .... name is Janet.

5. They .... in the classroom.   6. There are ten students in .... classroom.

7. .... is a picture .... the wall.

H.   You, your country, your city

1.   What is your name ?   ....

2.   What country are you from ?   ....

3.   What city are you from ?   ....

4.   Is your country hot ?   ....

5.   Is your city big or small ?   ....

6.   Is your city clean or dirty ?   ....

I. **The opposite of**

1. Small .....   2. Cold .....   3. Black .....

4. Dirty .....   5. Yes .....

J. **Say the Alphabet**

A B C ... etc.

K. **What is the letter ?**

1. Co_ntry _u_   2. Bo_rd _a_   3. Wh_te   4. Stud_nt _e_

5. Opp_site _o_   6. Teac_er _h_   7. Ei_ht _g_   8. Bra_il _z_

9. Twel_e ✓   10. Vo_el _w_

L. **What are the days of the week ?**

1. Sunday

2. Monday

3. Tuesday

4. Wednesday

5. Thursday

6. Friday

7. Saturday

M. **between, before, and after**

1. Sunday is _after_ Saturday.   2. _Tuesday_ is before Wednesday.

3. _Thursday_ is after Wednesday.   4. N is between ..._M_... and ..._O_...

5. Twelve is between ..._eleven_.. and ..._thirteen_..   6. X is _before_ Y

7. Z is.._after_.Y

Spelling tests unit 1

A.

pencil	chair	picture	table	tight
wall	ceiling	teacher	woman	window

B.

my	your	floor	her	student
they	there	name	classroom	what

C.

one	two	three	four...etc. up to ten	
eleven	twelve	thirteen	fourteen... etc. up to twenty	

D.

face	nose	ears	mouth	hair
under	left	right	opposite	alphabet

Unit 2

A. **What are the months of the year?**

1. January
2. Hebruary
3. March
4. April
5. May
6. ~~Saty~~ June
7. ~~August~~ July
8. August
9. september
10. October
11. November
12. December

B. **A or an ?**

1. It is an animal.
2. She is a student.
3. A cat is a small animal.
4. An elephant is a big animal.
5. There is an umbrella on the floor.

C. **What is your address**

134 Latimer
Beaconsfield Road
London   SZ/7 1EP

D. **What is the time in words ?**

5.00 ....

6.30 ....

8.15 ....

2.45 ....

1.50 ....

11.25 ....

E. **Colours**

1. The board is ....
2. The walls are ....
3. The floor is ....
4. The table is ....
5. My chair is ....
6. My eyes are ....
7. My hair is ....
8. My shoes are ....
9. The door is ....

F. **What is the plural of ...**

1. Book ....   2. Chair ....   3. Table ....

4. Man ....   5. Woman ....   6. Person ....

G. **What is the word?**

1. My mother and father are my ....

2. There are five people in my ....

3. She is six months old, she is a ....

4. He is eight years old, he is a .....*boy*.................

5. She is eight years old, she is a .....*ch*...............

6. She is sixteen years old, she is a ....

H. **to have**

1. I .....*have*.....a pen.   2. You .....*have* ~~are~~.........long hair.

3. She .....*has*........ green eyes.   4. He ....*has*........a black bag.

5. The classroom .....*has*......four walls.   6. We ....*have*.....a big classroom.

I. **What are the words ?**

Masato is ....*a*........ student. He is ......*from*...... Japan. He ....*has*........ long, black hair

.....*and*....... brown eyes. He is not .....~~go to~~ *at*...... school today. He is .....~~at~~ *at*...... home.

His house .....*has*......... a big garden. There .....~~There~~ *is*...... a swimming pool in the garden.

J. **What is the question word ?**

1. .....*where*.....are you from ?   2. .....*what*.....is your name ?

    I am from Italy.   My name is Paulo.

3. .....*How many*..pictures are there in the classroom ?   4. .....*Are*..... you a student ?

    There are six pictures.   Yes, I am a student.

5. ....*Is*... she your teacher ?   6. .....*Which*.. day is after Friday ?

    No, she is not my teacher.   Saturday is after Friday.

7. ....*Do*...... you have a computer ?   8. .....*Does*... he have a car ?

    No, I do not have a computer.   Yes, he has a car.

K. **Correct these sentences.**

eg. The table are blue.   The table <u>is</u> blue..

    I am teacher   I am <u>a</u> teacher.

1. He have long hair.   ....

2. He has a telephone on his car. ....

3. They are in home. ....

4. There is a umbrella on the chair. ....

5. They have big house. ....

Spelling tests unit 2

A.

1. opposite	2. Wednesday	3. which	4. hair
5. yellow	6. trousers	7. shirt	8. eyes
9. short	10. white		

B.

1. England	2. mouse	3. country	4. between
5. before	6. grey/gray	7. shoes	8. answer
9. telephone	10. brother		

C.

1. city	2. dirty	3. letter	4. week
5. umbrella	6. orange	7. green	8. question
9. telephone	10. father		

D.

1. February	2. autumn	3. address	4. minute
5. whose	6. quarter	7. computer	8. does
9. children	10. regular		

Unit 3

A. What is the job ?

1. T _ _ _ _ _ r   2. P _ _ _ _ _ _ _ n

3. D _ _ _ _ r   4. D _ _ _ _ _ t

5. S _ _ _ _ _ _ _ y   6. T _ _ _   D _ _ _ _ _

B. What is the sentence ?

eg. There/ four pictures / the wall.   There <u>are</u> four pictures <u>on</u> the wall.

1. He/brown hair/blue eyes.   …………...…..............……..

2. It/pencil.   …………...…...........

3. I/a computer/home.   …………...…...........

4. My mother/teacher.   …………...….................

5. What/taxi driver/use/his job ? …………...…...............

C. What do they use ?

1. A teacher uses ……………...…   2. A secretary uses …..................

3. A policeman uses …..................   4. Taxi drivers use …..................

5. Students use …..................

D. What is the word ?

1. …………….…use a book in the classroom.

2. …………….… don't use the board.

3. …………….… doesn't use a computer in his/her job.

4. My …………….… uses his computer at home.

5. …………….… don't use guns in England.

E.

1. My house

    My house …..… three bedrooms, one living …..… and …..… bathroom. There …..… a bath
    in the bathroom, but …..… isn't a shower. ? My house …..… a small garden.

2. My room

    My room ……..… white walls. There are pictures ……..… the walls. I have a television
    ……..… a computer in my room. ……..… is a table between the bed and the door.
    There is a telephone ………..… the table.

Adrian kee *I does*

F.   Come or go ?

1.   He .... home after school.

2.   I .... to school from Monday to Friday.

3.   We .... to the pub on Saturdays.

4.   We don't .... to school on Sundays.

5.   Do you usually .... to the cinema on Saturday ?

A

G.   What do you prefer ?

a.   <u>Animals</u>

1.   I like ....…

2.   I don't like ....…

3.   I prefer .... to …..................…

b.   <u>Food</u>

1.   I like ....…

2.   I don't like ....…

3.   I prefer .... to ....…

c.   <u>Drinks</u>

1.   I like ....…

2.   I don't like ....…

3.   I prefer .... to ....…

H.   What is the negative ?

eg.   He likes tea.   He <u>doesn't</u> like tea.

1.   He uses a computer.   He doesn't uses a computer

2.   We have a car.   we don't have a car

3.   There is a swimming pool in the garden. There is't a ew

4.   She has blue eyes.   She *dom't* ~~has~~ blue eyes

5.   I think this food is nice.   I think this food is nice
                                                         don't

I.   In the classroom, what things are ...

1.	big ?	....	2.	clean ?	....
3.	dirty ?	Adrian Guser	4.	blue ?	Teacher book
5.	brown ?	rinda hair	6.	black ?	MY Trousute

지가 쓰다
Picter Frame

J. **Spell the plurals**

1. Man _men_   2. Woman _women_

3. Person _people_   4. Child _children_

5. Mouse _mouses_

K. **Food and Drink**

What do you usually have...

1. for breakfast ? _I usually have orange juice_   2. for lunch ? _I usually have meat rice and beans_

3. for dinner ? _I usually have fish_

When do you usually have...

4. a sandwich ? _I usually have for lunch_   5. toast ? _I usually have for breakfast_

6. wine ? _I usually have for dinner_   7. coffee ? _I usually have for breakfast_

L. **What do we sometimes / usually / always / never do ?**

1. I _usually_ come to school on Mondays.

2. I _never_ come to school on Sundays.

3. The teacher _never_ speaks my language in the classroom.

4. We _always_ speak English in the classroom.

5. I _sometimes_ drink wine with my dinner.

6. I _usually_ go to the pub after school.

M. **Read these sentences. What do you sometimes / usually / always / never do ?**

1. I never listen to _pop_ (music)

2. I usually have .... for breakfast.

3. I always have _coffee_ with/without sugar.

4. I usually drink _water_ with my dinner.

5. I sometimes go to _the Pub_ after school.

6. I usually listen to _He_ music.

N. **Where do the words go ?**

1. I have breakfast before I come to school.
   (usually) ....

2. I always go in the mornings.
   (to school) ....

3. I have lunch at home.
   (never) ....

4. He sometimes goes after school.

    (to the pub)...

5. I don' t have cereal for breakfast.

    (on Sundays)..

O. What are the questions for these words ?

eg. you/eat/home ? = <u>Do</u> you eat <u>at</u> home ?

1. you/ever/watch television ?   ....

2. they/ever/come/school/by bus ?   ....

3. students/ever/eat lunch/the classroom ? ....

4. she/ever/listen/radio ?   ....

5. we/ever/have a lesson/Sunday ?   ....

P. Correct these sentences

1. I have usually eggs for breakfast.   2. He watch sport on TV.

3. I like watch the news.   4. I favourite kind of music is Classical music.

5. I am prefer pop music to jazz.   6. There is a good film in TV.

7. She understand our language.   8. I not like his friends.

9. There have ten students in the classroom. 10. We don't eat cereal at the morning.

Q. What are the words ?

1. This computer .... easy to use. It is the same .... my computer ....home.

2. He has ....same colour hair as his brother, but his eyes ....a different colour.

3. I generally watch ....news in the evening, but sometimes .... is difficult to understand.

R. Are these words adjectives, verbs or nouns ?

green	right	ask	long	garden
use	shower	prefer	favourite	bad
think	thing	sugar	come	afternoon

Adjectives: Verbs: Nouns:

....

....

....

....

....

Unit 3 spelling test

A.

1.	teacher	2.	bathroom	3.	bedroom	4.	without
5.	bread	6.	horrible	7.	quite	8.	England
9.	speak	10.	so				

B.

1.	chairs	2.	adult	3.	mouse	4.	child
5.	this	6.	these	7.	here	8.	there
9.	breakfast	10.	language				

C.

1.	favourite	2.	listen	3.	watch	4.	understand
5.	easy	6.	difficult	7.	usually	8.	different
9.	restaurant	10.	always				

D.

1.	secretary	2.	adjective	3.	thing	4.	think
5.	nationality	6.	afternoon	7.	sometimes	8.	same
9.	generally	10.	bread				

Unit 4

A. Present Simple and Present Continuous

Write one sentence in the **present simple** and one sentence in the **present continuous** using these words.

1. He/listen/radio.

   ....

   ....

2. She/use/computer.

   ....

   ....

3. He/watch/TV.

   ....

   ....

4. I/sit/chair.

   ....

   ....

5. She/study/English.

   ....

   ....

B. These sentences are wrong. What is the right sentence ?

1. I never listen the radio.   I never listen to the radio
2. He from Brazil.   He is from Brazil
3. Do you have a umbrella ?   Do you have an umbrella ?
4. The London is dirty.   London is dirty
5. I think this picture nice.   I think this picture is nice.
6. It is very a good film.   It is a
7. I no understand this word.   I don't understand this word
8. He not listening to the teacher.   He is not listen to the teach
9. Do you watching TV ?   Do you watch TV ?
10. Are you ever study at home ?   Do you ever study at home ?

C. Numbers Say these numbers.

a. 16   b. 60   c. 33   d. 77   e. 109

f. 555   g. 1,280   h. 20,000   i. 250,000   j. 60,000,000

D. **Give three examples of...**

Fruit ....

Vegetables ....

Meat ....

Colours ....

Animals ....

E. **What is the word ?**

1. He .... reading a newspaper.

2. She .... not understand English newspapers.

3. He has a lot .... friends in this city.

4. I write postcards .... my friends.

5. Do .... read magazines ?

F. **Use a gerund**

1. I like *living* in London.

2. They like *reading* English.

3. She likes *going* to the cinema.

4. I don't like *watching* television in the morning, I prefer *listening* to the radio.

5. I prefer *going* to school in the morning.

G. **Where do you put these things ?**

1. Money	2. Keys	3. Wallet
4. Telephone numbers	5. Your book after the lesson	6. Dirty clothes
7. Your coat	8. Stamps	9. Letters

*I eat
You eat
He she it ―*

H. **What are the words ?**

Joe *goes* to school in the morning. He has breakfast ....*at*.. home, and he *drinks* a cup of coffee at school. He likes studying, and always listens ...*to*... the teacher, but sometimes he .*doesn't*. *does* *t* understand. Sometimes he ...*goes* to the cinema after school.

doesn't

I. **Write sentences in the** Present Simple **with these verbs.**

1. Have ....

2. Know ....

3. Watch ....

4. Eat ....

5. Drink ....

6. Understand ....

J. **Write sentences in the** Present Continuous **with these verbs.**

1. Study ....

2. Watch ....

3. Listen ....

4. Read ....

5. Write ....

6. Teach ....

K. **Questions and Negatives**

<u>What is the question word ?</u>   <u>What is the negative answer ?</u>

1. Does he ...... English ?   No..

2. Is he ...... to the teacher ?   No..

3. .... she like going to the cinema ?   No..

4. Do they .... to school in the morning ?   No..

5. ...... he reading ..... English newspaper ?   No..

L. **Correct these sentences**

1. Do you like go to the cinema ?   2. He like going to the cinema.

3. We like going the cinema.   4. I like going to cinema.

5. He is listen to the radio.   6. We are listening the radio.

7. They are listening to radio.   8. She listening to the radio.

M. **What is the sentence ?**

1. I/eat/lot/bread.   ....

2. There/about/60 million people/Britain.   ....

3. What/happening/that classroom ?   ....

4. I/from/Scotland/but/live/London.   ....

5. I/not/know/lot/people/this city.   ....

6. There/lot/student/classroom.   ....

N. **Sentences in the Present Simple**

1. What kind of music .....*do*........ you .../*listen*.... to ? (to listen)

2. ...*Does*...... he ...*Prefer*.... coffee or tea ? He ...*Prefer*..... coffee. (to prefer)

3. .....*Do*......... you usually .....*go*......... home by bus ? (to go)

4. ......*Are*.... you a teacher or a student ? I ......*am*...... a student. (to be)

5. Where .....*does*..... she ....*have*...... lunch ? She ....*has*... lunch at home. (to have)

6. ....*Does*.. John ...*teach*..... you English ? Yes, he ...*teaches* me English. (to teach)

O. **Sentences in the Present Continuous**

1. .....*Are*.. you .../*listening* to me or the radio ? (to listen)

2. She .....*is*.. ....*eating* lunch. (to eat)

3. What .....*are*..... they ...*doing*....? (to do) They *are*.......*studying*.... at school. (to study)

4. ....*is*...... she ....*drinking* beer ? No, she ....*is*......... ...*not*.... beer, but she ....*like*....... ....*drink* cider. (to drink)

5. Which language ...*are*....... they ...*speaking* ? They ..*are*......... *speaking* Spanish. (to speak)

Unit 4 spelling test

A.

because	wrong	vegetables	fruit
address	pocket	example	prefer
listening	thirty		

B.

right	write	chicken	lettuce
eight	eighty	eighteen	friend
magazine	wallet		

C.

thousand	carrot	favourite	newspaper
keys	call	know (verb)	dance
million	meat		

Unit 5

A. Prepositions

1. I work ...... the day.

2. I usually sleep .... about seven hours.

3. He sleeps during the day because he works .... night.

4. I like listening .... the radio .... the morning, but I prefer watching TV .... the evening.

5. He doesn't like cooking .... home. He prefers eating .... restaurants.

6. We don't work .... Sundays.

7. She likes bread .... soup.

8. The teacher never sits down .... the lesson.

B. Countable or Uncountable ?   Correct these sentences.

1. I don't eat a lot of rices. ....

2. I have two hundreds dollar. ....

3. I like different kinds of musics. ....

4. The news are on TV in the evening. ....

5. My money are in my wallet. ....

6. This trousers are new. ....

7. He has black hairs and blue eye. ....

C. What is the sentence ?

1. I/keep/knives/forks/drawer. ....

2. I/usually/glass/wine/dinner. ....

3. He/sometimes/bowl/cereal/breakfast. ....

4. There/five/clean/shirt/wardrobe. ....

D. What are the words ?

I like cooking .... home. I have .... nice, big kitchen with a .... of cupboards, a good cooker, a microwave .... a small table. I can eat in .... kitchen. I .... eat my breakfast there, but I prefer .... dinner in the living room. I don't .... doing the washing up.

E.   Use an adverb: well   badly   quickly   slowly

1.   I like using a microwave because it cooks food ....

2.   I know him ....

3.   I always eat hot soup ....

4.   When it is very hot, I usually sleep …

F.   What are the words ?

I like playing chess, but I can't play .... well. I always play quite slowly because

.... think a lot .... the game. I want .... play well, so I am .... some books

about chess. I am learning a lot .... new things, but not very quickly, because ....

is very difficult.

G.   What can/can't you do quite/very well?

eg.   use a compter   <u>I can</u> use a computer <u>quite well</u>.

1.   play football   ....

2.   speak English   ....

3.   dance   ....

4.   sing   ....

5.   speak your language   ....

6.   cook   ....

H.   Put prepositions in these sentences.

1.   I always have a coffee .... coming to school.

2.   It is difficult to live in a country .... knowing the language.

3.   I always do the washing up .... eating dinner.

4.   Sometimes I work for two hours .... sitting down.

5.   .... playing tennis I always have a shower.

6.   I can't understand the newspaper .... using a dictionary.

I.   Infinitive verbs

Write 12 **infinitive verbs**.

1.   ....   2.   ....   3.   ....

4.   ....   5.   ....   6.   ....

7.   ....   8.   ....   9.   ....

10.   ....   11.   ....   12.   ....

J. **Write sentences/questions with the verb 'want'.**

1. You/play/football/ ? ....

2. He/not/work hard. ....

3. I/buy/new clothes. ....

4. How many hours/you/study? ....

5. I/listen/music. ....

K. **What are the right words ?**

1. I want .... new clothes.

2. Do you .... sugar in your tea ?

3. They want .... make a chocolate cake, but they don't know how.

4. Q. .... wants this apple ?

   A. I want it !

5. We .... want to learn any new words.

6. I don't think the baby .... to eat this.

7. I want .... speak English well.

9. She usually wants .... drink after working for four hours.

10. How many lessons does the student .... ?

L. **Some, any, an , a**

1. They've got .... food in the fridge.

2. We haven't got .... meat, but we can cook .... potatoes.

3. Have you got .... Michael Jackson CDs ? I've got .... Michael Jackson CD.

4. Have you got .... brothers and sisters ? Yes, I've got two sisters and .... brother.

5. I haven't got............ money so can you give me .... money ?

Unit 5 spelling tests

A.

1. during	2. night	3. minute	4. lesson
5. soup	6. cook	7. kitchen	8. fridge
9. freezer	10. ice-cream		

B

1. glass	2. plate	3. bowl	4. cupboard
5. wardrobe	6. drawer	7. clothes	8. saucepan
9. quick	10. downstairs		

C

1. preposition	2. infinitive	3. hungry	4. thirsty
5. foot	6. feet	7. thumb	8. toe
9. shirt	10. skirt		

D

1. gloves	2. dress	3. pair	4. some
5. any	6. young	7. teenager	8. expensive
9. cheap	10. closed		

Unit 6

A. **Possessive adjectives** *my, your, his, her, its, our, their*

1. He is a student and that is ...*His*.... book.

2. She is a taxi-driver and that is ...*her*... car.

3. They are students and these are...*their*.. books

4. I am a dancer and these are ...*my*... shoes.

5. The cat is hungry but there isn't any food in ...*It's*... bowl.

6. I know you study at this school, but who is ...*your*.. teacher ?

7. We want to give ...*our*... mother a new dress for ..*our*... birthday.

8. They want to give ...*Their*.. father a new jacket for ..*His*.... birthday.

Bi. **Whose ... ?** **Use these words to make questions with *whose*.**

eg.	Whose ...	(pen/that)	Whose pen is that ?
1.	Whose....	(money/this)	*whose money is this* ?
2.	Whose...	(shoes/those)	*whose shoes is those* ?
3.	Whose...	(socks/these)	*whose socks is these* ?
4.	Whose...	(wine/it)	*whose wine is it* ?

Bii. **Now put in some words to make questions.**

6. Whose book ...*whose book is that*... ?

7. Whose pictures ...*whose pictures is those* ?

8. Whose bag ...*whose bag is that*... ?

9. Whose gloves *whose gloves is these*

10. Whose scarf ...*whose scarf is that*?

C. **Syllables** **How many syllables are there in these adjectives ?**

small	(1)	dirty	( )
beautiful	( )	big	( )
difficult	( )	soft	( )
hard	( )	easy	( )

D.   **Comparatives**

Make comparatives **from these** adjectives.

cold.....   hard.....   soft.....   nice.....   slow.....

easy.........   quick.....   dirty.........   happy.........   tall.....

E.   **Comparatives**   **Write a comparative adjective in the space.**

1.   London is .... than Oxford.

2.   I think my shoes are .... than his shoes.

3.   The floor is .... than the ceiling.

4.   Wine is usually .... than Champagne.

5.   July is .... than January in England.

6.   It is .... to spell 'pen' than 'possessive'.   *Joe*

7.   I can sleep on the floor, but I prefer my bed because it is ....

F.   **Someone, something, anyone, or anything**

1.   ...*Someone*... is waiting for you in the office. He wants to talk to you about ...*Something*...

2.   I don't know ...*anyone*... taller than my brother.

3.   There is ...*Something*... on your shoe.

4.   There isn't ...*anyone*..... here who plays golf.

5.   Is there *anything* in the cupboard ?

6.   I don't like parties when I don't know ...*anyone*... and there isn't ...*anything*... nice to eat.

G.   **Give two examples of...**

Something you write with.   ......*Pen*......   ......*✗*......

Someone English you know.   ....*Anna*   ....*Anna*

Something we keep in a drawer.   ....

Something you can make.   ....

Something you don't like doing.   ....

Someone older than you.   ....

H. Have and have got

Write these sentences using **have got**.

eg. Do you have a car ?   **Have** you **got** a car ?

1. I don't have any time to study. ....

2. Does she have long hair ? ....

3. He has a good job. ....

4. I don't have a visa for the U.S.A. ....

5. Do we have any rice at home ? ....

6. Does she have any friends in London. ....

8. He doesn't have any brothers or sisters. ....

I. Well, good and good at

We don't usually say: He sings well.
We usually say : He is good at singing.   or   He is a good singer.
Change these sentences to something we usually say.

1. He cooks well.   .... cooking.

2. She teaches well.   .... teacher.

3. My mother and father dance well. .... dancing.

4. Can he cook well ?   .... cook.

5. She skis well.   .... skiing.

6. They work well.   .... workers.

7. My brother plays football well. .... football.

J. Is there an 's' or not ?

1. There are five Avalon book.

2. I listen to a lot of different kind of musics.

3. She never ask any question after the lesson.

4. She is twenty-five and she has four childrens.

5. Our teacher never sit on her chair.

6. Does he comes to school in the morning ?

7. I alway buys apple at the supermarket.

8. I don't read any English newspaper.

9. Why don't you likes vegetable ?

10. I know someone who live in Paris.

K. **Do you know these things from the first six units of Book One ?**

Correct these sentences.

1. Are they usually study in this classroom ? *Do they usually study in this classroom?*

2. My brother is sometimes listening classical music. *My brother is sometimes listen to ~*

3. My sisters is older me, but I am taller than him. *at taller her*

4. I've got any money, but it is home. *Some at*

5. Do you friends in London ? *Yes. my friends in London.* *have any ne*

6. Foreign language is easier learning when you are young.

7. What are you usually having for breakfast ? *I*

8. Do she have got some brother or sisters? *Does any*
   Has she got.

L. **Which words can go at the end of these sentences ?**

1. I have three children. Two sons and a ..*.du*........... .

2. I am not very good at ...*studying*.. .

3. In Australia, December is not in winter but in .*Summer*... .

4. This year, I want to go abroad on ...*# Itari*...... .

5. I like going to the beach, but I never swim in the ....*Sea*........ .

6. Sometimes I use the bus, but I prefer the train because it is ...*fast ca*........

7. My friend can't speak English, but she can speak French very ...*well*........... .

M. **The prepositions in these sentences are wrong. Write the right ones.**

1. There is never anything to do *at* <u>on</u> the weekend in this city.

2. We are going *to* <u>at</u> the nightclub by taxi.

3. I take the pen out <u>from</u> my pocket when I write *on* <u>to</u> the board.

4. My friend is in the USA *in* <u>at</u> this week.

5. *at* <u>In</u> the end of the lesson, the teacher says 'Goodbye' to the students.

6. I know the names of the students *n* <u>of</u> my class.

7. When he makes something nice <u>to</u> dinner, he usually gives something <u>at</u> me.

8. I don't like watching <u>to</u> the TV when I have friends *to* <u>in</u> my house. *at*

Unit 6 spelling tests

A.

begin	beach	beginning	married
anything	easier	daughter	no one
hotter	holiday		

B.

round	rain	wife	heavier
weather	square	snow	anyone
hard	beautiful		

C.

see (verb)	hear (verb)	something	happier
triangle	mountain	slowly	foreign
abroad	fast		

D.

mountain	bigger	river	enjoy
husband	dirtier	nothing	cloud
wind	someone		

Unit 7

A.   What did they do before ?

Change these sentences from the **Present Simple** to the **Past Simple**.

eg.   He works in a bank. (Last year/shop)   Last year he worked in a shop.

1.   She plays the guitar well. (Five years ago/badly)

....*Five years ago she played in a badly*....

2.   He wants a cigarette from me. (Yesterday/pen)

....*Yesterday He wanted a pen from me*....

3.   He watches a lot of films. (Last night/Titanic)

....*Last night He watched   Titanic*....

4.   He studies very hard. (Last weekend/12 hours)

....*Last weekend He studied for 12 hours*....

B.   Questions and Negatives in the past

Put these questions and negatives in the **Past Simple**.

1.   He doesn't like the colour of the shirt.   *He didn't liked the a*

2.   Does he live with you ?   *Did he live with you ?*

3.   Do they cook a lot of pasta ?   *Did they cook a lot of pasta ?*

4.   I don't listen to the radio.   *I didn't listen to the radio*

5.   Does he walk to school ?   *Did he walke to school ?*

6.   Where does she work ?   *Where did she worke ?*

C.   What is the Simple Past of these verbs ?

Understand	*Understood*	Teach	*Teaches*
Come	*Came*	Go	*went*
Read	*Reads*	Have	*had*
Wear	*wore wore*	Teach	*Teaches*
Think	*Thank Thought*	Know	*Knew*
Write	*wrote*	Forget	*Forgot*

D.   Correct these sentences in the Past Simple.

1.   I understanded his question.   *I was understooded his question.*

2.   I didn't understood anything during the lesson yesterday.

3.   She wores a very nice, blue dress.
                              She

4.   She didn't wore her red skirt.   *She didn't ware her red skirt.*

5.   A different teacher teached us yesterday.   *A different teacher.*

6.   Did you spoke to your mother last night ?

7.   Where did you went yesterday ?

8.   He buyed some chocolates in the newsagents and gave them to me.

9.   Did they liked the film ?

10.   We drank a lot at the party, so we comed home in a taxi.

E.   Make Past Simple questions

1.   You/go out/last night ?   *Did you go out last night*

2.   He/forget/bring/book ?   *Did   ~   his book?*

3.   How many/letter/he write/yesterday ?   *How many did*

4.   When/you come/London ?   *When did you came did London ?*

5.   Where/they have/dinner/last night ?   *Where did they had dinner last night?*

6.   What/you think about/film ?   *What did you think about film?*

F.   The verb 'to be' in the Past Simple

Put these sentences and questions in the Past Simple.

e.g. I am tired today.   I was tired yesterday.

1   He isn't very happy.   .... last Saturday.

2.   Are you hungry ?   ....this morning ?

3.   Is he at home ?   ....when you called ?

4.   The film isn't very good.   ....last night.

5.   Is the weather nice ?   ....during your holiday ?

6.   Is it cold ?   ....last week ?

7.   Are they abroad ?   ....last Christmas ?

8.   The cat is in the garden.   ....when I came home.

G.   Which goes with which ?

1.   He didn't sleep well...   ...to drink anything.

2.   They went to...   ...on the menu.

3.   We didn't want...   ...at work.

4.   She usually wears those shoes...   ...last night.

5.   I didn't like anything...   ...three weeks ago.

6.   They talked ...   ... for three hours.

7.   They were on holiday ...   ...bed early.

H. **Correct these sentences.**

1. He didn't was thirsty this morning.

2. She didn't go out in last night.

3. They didn't went to the party.

4. They didn't at home yesterday.

5. Did she enjoy the film at Saturday.

6. Did you go at the park ?

7. Which car did they preferred ?

8. She wasn't understand anything when she came to the school.

9. Did you late for school this morning ?

I. **Write the words**

1st.	*first*	2nd.	*second*	3rd.	*third*
4th.	*fourth*	5th.	*fifth*	6th.	*sixth*
7th.	*seventh*	8th.	*eighth*	9th.	*ninth*

J. **Correct these sentences.**

1. What your name ? *what is your name ?*

2. My teacher hair is blond and his eyes are brown.

3. I think my language is easy than this language.

4. A taxi is quicker that a bus, but a bus is cheaper.

5. He always buys me expensive something for Christmas.

6. Do you have anything is cold to drink ?

7. When you begin Book Two, you can give this book for your friend.

8. There is something I want ask you.

9. I don't like beer. I prefer to wine.

10. My father is in the living room seeing TV.
   watching

K. **Can and could**

Make a sentence using **can/can't** and **could/couldn't**.

e.g. When I was five I couldn't read a newspaper but now I can.

When I was sixteen I could swim 1000m, but now I can't.

1. When I was *twelve I could run 100m* .... but now I *now I can't* .

2. When I was *1 I couldn't ride* .... but now I ....

3. When I was .... but now I ....

4. When I was .... but now I ....

L. Questions

Make questions beginning with these words.

Does   *Does your family have say Does she have a Book*

Did   *Did you play Pootball in yestday* ?

How many   *How many your family?* ?

Is there   *Is there are* ?

Can   *Can you play tennis* ?

Could   *Could tell me where is ter Parkinan* ?

M. Prepositions for times

Which is the right preposition ? In some sentences there is not a preposition.

1.   I don't work *on* Sundays.

2.   Her birthday is *on* June 3rd.

3.   You usually call me *at* the weekend.

4.   He works *in* the morning, and studies *in* the afternoon.

5.   I can't go out *at* this evening because I don't have any money.

6.   She couldn't work *in* the evenings, because she had a young child.

7.   When I can't sleep *at* night, I read a book and have a glass of milk.

8.   I didn't understand anything *in* my first day at this school.

9.   In our country, it doesn't usually rain *in* summer.

10.   I didn't come to school ...... last week.

Unit 7 spelling tests

A.

science	geography	taught	thought
bought	remember	fourth	fifth
eighth	present		

B.

wore	spoke	understood	boring
forget	spelt	could	death
finish	meant		

Unit 8

A. Future Simple

These sentences with **will** are wrong. Make them right.

1. Do you will come to school tomorrow ? ~~will~~ you come ~
2. I don't will see John tonight. I 'll *won't* see ~
3. I will *be* to study harder. I
4. Will you ~~to~~ have dinner with us tonight. you will ~
5. When will she gets up ?
6. Will you are rich in the future ? will
7. I not will go to bed early tonight. I won't .
8. It will *be* rain tomorrow.
9. I will here tomorrow.
10. I'm will be tired after the lesson.

B. Different Tenses

Make sentences from these words. Put them in the right tense - **Present Simple, Past Simple**, or **Future Simple**. The words in **bold** will help you.

1. He/eat/a lot of chips/**last night**. He is *ate* eat a lot of ~
2. She/come/to school/**tomorrow**. She will come ~
3. It/**always**/rain/*on* my birthday. It is
4. She/**often**/forget/people's names. She often *forgot* ~
5. He/ask/us/some questions/**soon**. He will ask us some questions soon

C. Questions in The Future Simple

Make questions with these words.

1. You/come/here tomorrow ? Will you come here tomorrow ?
2. You/think/she/like/ film tonight ? Do you think she will like film tonight ? Will she lik the film ?
3. How many/people/go/the party ? How many people will go the party
4. You/ask her after the lesson ? ~~You will~~ will you
5. You/here/in three weeks' time ? *be* You
6. The school/open/next Monday ? The school
   will be o

D. **Negatives in the Future Simple**
Use **won't**, and a **verb**.

1. We ...won't... _be_ ... late tomorrow.

2. I ...won't... _bring_ ... my book next lesson.

3. The teacher ...won't... _ask_ ... him difficult questions.

4. I ...won't... _send_ /_write_ you a lot of letters from England, because I will work and study every day.

5. Our teacher says the exam ...won't... _be_ ... very difficult.

6. She ...won't... _watch_ ... the film on TV tonight, because she watched it at the cinema and didn't like it.

7. I know he ...won't... _do_ ... the washing up after dinner - he never does it !

E. **Comparatives**

Write the right comparative form.

e.g.	big	bigger than		expensive	more expensive than
1.	tall	_taller than_	2.	rich	_richer than_
3.	interesting	_more interesting than_	4.	early	_earlier than_
5.	later	_later than_	6.	famous	_more famous than_
7.	soon	_sooner than_	8.	funny	_funnier than_

F. **Comparatives**

Complete these sentences with the **comparative** form of the adjective.

e.g. The table is .... the chair. (heavy)
The table is heavier than the chair.

1. England is ...Smaller than the Brazil... Brazil. (small)

2. Football players are ...richer than the teacher... teachers. (rich)

3. Tonight's film will be...more interesting than... the one yesterday. (interesting)

4. A burger is ...more cheaper than... a pizza. (cheap)

5. This picture is ...more beautifuler than... that one. (beautiful)

6. Russian is ...more difficulter than... English. (difficult)

7. Swimming is ...easier than... skiing. (easy)

G. **Subject and Object Pronouns**

Write the correct **pronouns** in this grammar table.

subject pronoun	object pronoun	subject pronoun	object pronoun
I	me	You	_You_
_He_	him	she	_Her_
it	_its_	we	_ us_
you	_You_	them	_them_

H. Subject and Object Pronouns

Answer these questions using pronouns.

e.g. Did <u>David and John</u> buy <u>the house</u> ? Yes, <u>they</u> bought <u>it</u>.

1. Did Mary call Simon ? Yes *she called him* .
2. Did you buy the little red car ? Yes *I bought it* .
3. Did those policemen see the women ? Yes *they saw them* .
4. Does the letter say that Damon likes Justine ? Yes *~~he liked to~~* .
5. Did Steven cook chicken for his children ? Yes *~~H~~he cooked chicke.for~~x~~ them*
6. Does your sister enjoy her English lesson ? No *~~she~~ Does't enjoied* .
7. Did you have that jacket two months ago ? Yes *I did have that* .
8. Have you got my glasses ? No *I haven't got my glasses* .

I. Possessive Adjectives and Possessive Pronouns

Write these sentences using a **possessive pronoun**.

e.g. They are <u>my shoes</u>. They are <u>mine</u>.

1. This is <u>my book</u>. This is *mine*
2. Where is <u>your book</u> ? Where is *yours*
3. I've got <u>your pen</u>. I've *got yours*.
4. The red house is <u>his house</u>. The *his*
5. The big car is <u>her car</u>. The *Hers*
6. You can use <u>our computer</u>. You *ours*
7. This is <u>their ball</u>. This *theirs*

J. Possessives and Comparatives.

Use a **possessive pronoun** or a **comparative**.

1. Your hair is *longer* than mine.
2. Their TV is bigger than *ours*.
3. His car is very fast, but I prefer *mine*.
4. I think your shoes are *bigger* than hers.
5. My Dad is *taller* than yours.
6. This pen is not working. Can I use *yours* ?
7. I can't give you this wine, because it's not *mine*.

K. Make these sentences right.

1. I am not use my computer now. *I am not useging my computer now*
2. I sometimes late for the lesson because of my job. *I am sometimes last the less*
3. He goes to job early in the morning. *He gos to job*.
4. Do you know anyone with car ? *Do you know anyone with a car ?*

© *Avalon Book Company Ltd., 1999*

5.   I went to school until I was eighteen years. old .

6.   They are usually come to our house at the weekend.

7.   I speak English slow, because I am a beginner.   I speak English slowly ~

8.   They speak English differently, because they American.

L.   Verbs with 'back'

Put in the correct verb, in the correct tense.

1.   Pedro gave me his pen during the lesson, but I forgot to .... give .... it back.

2.   I have bought you a shirt. If you don't like it, you can .... take . it back to the shop.

3.   I love this city, and I want to ...... come ...... back here one day.

4.   She is very happy here, and doesn't want to .... go .... back to her old job.

5.   I went to Milton Keynes last year. I will never ...... go .... back.

6.   You can use my calculator for your exam, but don't forget to .... give .. it back.

M.   Opposites

What is the **opposite** of …

to get up	To go to bed	late	early
asleep	awake	alive	dead
the past	the future	last week	next week
poor	rich	in front of	in behind of
come	go	begin	end

N.   Come, come back, go, go back

1.   I sometimes .... go .... to the cinema at the weekend.

2.   My parents ...... come back to Scotland last year on holiday, and they want to
      .... there next year.

3.   I didn't .... here yesterday.

4.   I will .... to my country in the summer.

5.   She .... here this morning, but .... home because she forgot
      her books.

6.   I like this school so I think I will .... com back .... next year.

O.   Who or what is…

(You can answer with **nothing** or **no one**.)

1. who .. sitting next to you ?   Sergio 자네

2.   … sitting opposite you ?   Ji Hyun

3. what is behind you ?   Nothing

4.   … opposite this school ?   (   )

5. *What's* next to the school ?   ..Pub...Caff.........

6. *who* ... sitting near you ?   ...Sergio...*Bid* sitting near me.

7. *Who's* living with you ?   ..frieder...............

8. *what's* ... behind your house ?   ....

9. *who's* ... between you and the door ?   ....

P. Make these sentences right.

1. I was not wake at 9.00 this morning, but I was asleep.

2. He asleep for six hours last night.

3. Mozart was die more than 200 years ago.

4. There is a pub nearly my house.

5. There are two televisions to my house.

6. I think you will be cry when you watch that film.

7. He is very funny. I am always laugh when I am with him.

8. I don't have my book today. I don't bring it.

Gi Hyun

Sergio

Q. Different tenses

Make sentences from these words. Put them in the right tense - **Present Simple**, **Past Simple**, **Future Simple**. The words in **bold** will help you.

1. We/make/a pizza/for her/**a week ago**.   *we ma* ....

2. I/**often**/eat/apple/lunch.   ....

3. My sister/late/dinner/**yesterday**.   ....

4. You/come/ school/**tomorrow**?   ....

Unit 8 spelling tests

A.

early	asleep	awake	alive
dead	opposite	almost	tomorrow
famous	through		

B.

across	difference	brought	laugh
bigger	tunnel	apostrophe	nearly
heard	kilometre		

Unit 9

A. Verb Forms

What are these **verb forms** ?

present	past	past participle
like	liked	liked
use	....	....
play	....	....
have	....	....
know	....	....
teach	....	....

B. The Present Perfect

Put in a word to make a sentence or question in the **Present Perfect**.

1. How long .... you been here ?
2. I .... taught English here for two years.
3. We .... known them for three years.
4. He has .... that car for about six years.
5. How long have they .... students at this school ?
6. I have not .... football for about a year.
7. He has not .... to our class for three weeks.
8. He .... been in Germany for a month.
9. We have .... this computer for two years.
10. The teacher has not .... any questions for about ten minutes.

C. For or Since ?

1. I have been here .....since..... three o'clock.
2. How many jobs have you had .....since..... 1995 ?
3. She has had that car .....since..... Christmas.
4. They have known us .....since..... eight years.
5. He has been unhappy .....since..... his first day in London.
6. I have used this book .....for since..... my first lesson at this school.
7. I have studied English .....for..... 2 years, ...since..... 1998.

D. Make these words into sentences in the Present Perfect.

1. They/live/here/December. .....They have lived here sinc December.....
2. I/know/them/about six months. .....I have known them for about six months.....
3. She/be/a student here/last August. .....She has been a student here sinc last Aus.....
4. They/have/that car/1975. .....They hada that car 197f.....

5. she/have/thatjob/2 years.   *she has had that job for 2 years* (handwritten)
6. I/teach/here/1994.   *I have teached here since 1994* (handwritten)
7. We/be/married/3years.   *we have been married 3 years for* (handwritten)

E.   Past Participles

I have seen Gradiater. (handwritten)

1. People say that film is good, but I haven't ......*seen*... it.   (see)   *saw*
2. People say she's a horrible person, but I have never ....*met*... her.   (meet) *met I have met my friends*
3. I have never ...*done*... anything very difficult in my life.   (do)
4. She's an old friend. I have ..*known*.. her for ten years.   (know) *I have know you for 2 months*
5. He has ..*forgotten*..his English, because he hasn't studied for ten years.   (forget)
6. He has ..*written*..thirteen letters to me since last year.   (write) *I has be forgete your name I has forgoten* (handwritten)
7. I have not ..*read*... any of his books.   (read)
8. I haven't ..*made*.. a cake since your last birthday.   (make)
9. She is very famous, and she has ...*had*... four husbands.   (have)
10. That has ..*been*... our favourite restaurant for twenty years.   (be)

F.   Present Perfect and Past Simple

Put the verb in brackets ( ) into the right tense.

1. I ...*came*... (to come) to London three weeks ago
2. I ..*have been*... (to be) in London for three weeks.
3. We ...*lived*... (to live) here since 1994.
4. She ...*lived*... (to live) with her sister last year, but now she lives here.
5. I ...*tried*... (to try) water-skiing on holiday in France last year.
6. I ..*have not eaten*.. (to eat, not) anything today, so I'm very hungry.
7. I ...*saw*... (to see) a film in that big cinema last year.
8. She ...*never tried*... (to try, never) this kind of coffee.

G.   Things we have done.

When we talk about things we have done *in our lives,* we use the Present Perfect.
With questions we use *ever*, and with negative sentences, we use *never*.

1. She/fly/in a plane.   *she has flied in a plane* (handwritten)
2. He/never/see/snow.   *He has never* (handwritten)
3. They/travel/to a lot of different countries.   ....
4. You/ever/eat/Turkish food ?   .... ?
5. She/meet/a lot of famous people.   ....
6. He/ever/play volleyball ?   .... ?

H. Give an example of:

1. A very good book you have read.

.... ?

2. Someone you have known for more than a year.

....

3. Something horrible you have eaten.

....

4. A famous film you have <u>never</u> seen.

....

5. A kind of food you have <u>never</u> eaten.

.... Hors ....

6. A country you have <u>never</u> been to.

....

I. Past Simple and Present Perfect

Remember that when we say the particular time something happened, we always use the Past Simple. Look at these examples:

I have eaten Italian food.   (no particular time)

I ate Italian food on holiday last year.   (particular time, on holiday last year)

Write sentences, using the right tense.

1. I/swim/in the sea.   *I've swum in the sea.*

   I/swim/in the sea last summer.   *I swam in the sea last summer*

2. He/meet/the president of Spain.   *He's met the president of Spain*

   He/meet/the president of Spain last summer.   *He met the president of Spain las s*

3. You/ever/eat/Thai/food ?   *Have you ever eaten Thai food ?*

   When you/eat/Thai/food ?   *When did you eat Thai food ?*

4. You/see/that new James Bond film ?   *Have you seen that new James Bond film*

   When/you/see/it ?   *When did you see it ?*

5. I/have/lunch.   *I've had lunch*

   I/have/lunch in a café yesterday.   *I had lunch in a café yesterda*

J. Irregular Verbs. Put in the verb forms.

see	*saw*	*seen*
break	*break*	*broken*
eat	ate	*eaten*
ride	rode	*ridden*
drive	*drive*	*driven*
write	wrote	*written*
read	*read*	read
know	*knew*	*known*
fly	flew	*flown*
drink	*drank*	*drunk*
swim	*swam*	*swum*
begin	began	*begun*

I see the you a desk

you saw the yesdday

I have seen last week

I saw him a mom

Have yeu eever seen a him

K. **Corrections**

Correct these questions and answers in the **Present Perfect**.

Been

1. How long you have studied here ?
   How long have you ✓ studied here

   I have been study here for two months.
   I have study for two months.
   been

2. How long do you know John ?
   How long have you ~~know~~ known John ?

   I have known him sincefive years.
   I have known him ~~since~~ five years

3. How long have you be in London ?
   How long have you

   I was be for three weeks here.
   I have been here

4. How long have she worked there ?
   How long has she worked there

   She has worked there in January.
   ....

L. **Adjectives, Comparatives, Superlatives**

adjective	comparative	superlative
hot	*hoter*	*hotest*
easy	*easyer*	*easist*
beautiful	*more beautifuler*	*most beautifulest*
difficult	*more difficult*	*most*
interesting	*more interest*	*more*
slow	*slow*	
expensive		
famous		
good	*best*	*best*
bad		

unit 9 spelling tests

A.

been	since	written	particular
eaten	ridden	bicycle	flew
better	ticket		

B.

opinion	capital	size	weight
height	biggest	world	thought
worse	worst		

Unit 10

A. Probably

Answer these questions, using the word **probably**.

1. What time will you go to bed tonight ?

....

2. What do you think the teacher does between lessons ?

....

3. When will you go back to your country ?

....

4. What kind of job will you do in the future ?

....

B. A life story

Complete these sentences with verbs in the **Past Simple**.

Herbert Jones 1906-1968.

Herbert Jones ..w.a.s.... born in East London in 1906. He .... to a school near his house until the age of 16. After that he .... in a shoe shop for twenty years. He (not) .... the work, and .... working as a taxi driver in 1942. When he .... 38 he .... his wife Fenella on holiday in Southend, and they .... married in a big church in East London. They .... together happily for many years, until he .... in 1968.

C. Adjectives

Make sentences with these words. Use the adjectives below.
important, necessary, nice, healthy, easier, dangerous, safe, polite

1. It isn't .... eat a lot of chocolate, crisps, and fizzy drinks.
2. It .... for me to learn English.
3. It isn't .... for children to play in the streets.
4. It .... take your passport when you go to another country.
5. It .... say 'please' when you ask for something.
6. It .... ride a motorbike without a seatbelt.
7. It .... to learn to swim than to ski.

D.   Choose have to or don't have to

1.   I can go to bed late tonight, because I .... get up early tomorrow.

2.   Everyone .... eat, but not everyone .... work.

3.   You .... wear a coat in summer.

4.   Students .... answer with a sentence, not one or two words.

5.   People who work in shops usually .... work on Saturday.

6.   After a comparative we .... use 'than'.

7.   My little sister .... go to school, but she doesn't like it.

8.   My grandfather .... pay for new glasses, because old people can get them free.

E.   Comparatives and Superlatives
Hotel Hawaii: 50m from the beach; £80 a night.
Hotel Benidorm: 100m from the beach; £50 a night.
Hotel Blackpool: 500m from the beach; £25 a night.

Now make a **comparative** or **superlative** from the adjective on the right..

1.   Hotel Benidorm is .... Hotel Hawaii.   (cheap)

2.   Hotel Blackpool is .... hotel.   (cheap)

3.   Hotel Hawaii is .... Hotel Benidorm.   (expensive)

4.   Hotel Hawaii is .... hotel.   (expensive)

5.   Hotel Benidorm is .... the beach .... Hotel Blackpool. (near)

6.   The .... hotel to the beach is Hotel Hawaii.   (near)

F.   Mistakes in the Present Perfect/Past Simple

1.   How long you have had that car ?
     I had it for six months.

     How long have you had that car?
     I have had it for six months

2.   Have you this job for a long time ?
     No, I have this job for two months.

     Have you had this job for a long time?
     No I have had this job for two months

3.   Where you have worked since last year ?
     I worked here since last year.

     Where have you worked since last year?
     I have worked here since last year

4.   Who did you meet since you came to London ?
     I have meet a lot of people since I came here.

     Who have you met since you came to London?
     I have met a lot of people since I came here.

G.   To go and to be in the present perfect

Choose **gone** or **been** for these sentences.

1.   My brother has .... to Japan but he came back last year.

2.   Where is Susan ? She has .... to the supermarket.

3. John went on a three-week holiday yesterday. Where has he .... ?

4. I've never .... to Korea.

H. Finish these sentences using the same + noun as ...

1. My friend is .... me.

2. An elephant is about .... a car.

3. London is about .... New York.

4. My mother is .... my father.

I. Write two examples of:

a. a fact ....

b. an opinion ....

J. Choose to be or to get + adjective.

1. I haven't eaten anything today. I am *get* .... very *hangr* ....

2. People *get* *tierd* .... when they don't sleep enough.

3. I *get* *eng* .... when people are rude.

4. I *am* *thistsy* .... Can I have a glass of water please?

5. Close the window please. I *got* *colal* ....

6. Old people often *get* *cold* .... in winter.

K. Use enough, not enough, too much or too many for these sentences.

1. I understand *enough* .... English to read a letter but I ~~not enough~~ *don't* know ~~too many~~ *enough* .... to write a letter.

2. There are *two many* .... cars in this city.

3. There is *too much* .... salt in this soup, it tastes horrible.

4. I have *enough* .... money to buy an old bicycle, but I *not enough* .... have *not enough* *don't* .... money to buy a new one.

5. My bag is big *enough* .... for your books.

L. Write sentences with to be going to.

1. I/play football this afternoon. *I am going to football this afternoon*

2. My friends/meet me in the pub. *my friends are going to meet me in the pub*

3. They/see the new film. *They are going to see the new film*

4. I/study English at home tonight. *I am going to study*

5. My mother/cook lasagne for lunch. *My mother is going to*

Unit 10 spelling exercises

A.

probably	packet	unhealthy	theatre
countryside	village	dangerous	helmet
choice	necessary		

B.

another	angry	enough	touch
cheque	company	factory	cough
ill	furniture		

Do not take the mickey out of the teacher

Index

(P17)

gestures

facial expressions

eye contact

body language

one shelf
shelves.

Man — Male
woman — female
sunba...

catek a

futu

fe   futu

funi